Paul Mellon:
Portrait of an Oil Baron

Other Books by William S. Hoffman

David: Report on a Rockefeller
The Stockholder
Sidney: The Poitier Story

Paul Mellon
Portrait of an Oil Baron

William S. Hoffman

Follett Publishing Company
Chicago

Manufactured in the United States of America.
Library of Congress Catalog Card Number: 74–80330
ISBN: 0–695–80503–7
First Printing

FOR PATRICIA AND ANDY

I'd like to thank Dwight and Barbara Steward, Shirley and Joe Konecny, John Hess, Paul Lawless, L. D. Shank, Jim Seligmann, and Joe Smyth, all of whom provided important help on this book.

One

INDUSTRIAL SOCIETY AS WE KNOW IT COULD NOT EXIST without oil. Huge armies could not march, mighty ships could not sail, great cities could not be lighted. Oil heats homes, runs automobiles, powers factories. Oil helps produce the clothes people wear, the food they eat, the homes they live in. Oil is indispensable in the Twentieth Century.

Seven major oil companies—Exxon, Texaco, Gulf, Mobil, Standard Oil of California, British Petroleum, Royal Dutch Shell—dominate the business. The "Seven Sisters" control seventy percent of the world's non-Communist oil market, and there is virtually no competition among these giants.

On February 20, 1974, a U.S. Senate subcommittee on multinational corporations revealed that *forty years earlier,* in 1934, the Seven Sisters drew up "one of the most explicit detailed cartel agreements ever written." The cartel included the "limiting of production to prop up prices," "maintaining prices in each market," and "obtaining the consent of other companies for a member's advertising budget in each market."

The energy crisis, primarily promoted by the Seven Sisters, cost some one million jobs in its first six months. People sat in endless lines waiting to get to a gas pump. Prices of hundreds of energy-related items skyrocketed. Utilities urged customers to turn down their thermostats, and when customers complied the utilities asked for rate increases, contending that profits were down.

Living costs in Philadelphia were typical of what was happening nationwide. Regular gasoline went from 40 cents a gallon in October, 1973, to 52 cents a gallon in March, 1974. Premium went from 44.3 cents to 56 cents. Heating oil leaped from 21.5 cents to 34 cents a gallon. Heating costs for a small ranch home jumped from $322.50 to $510.00.

The House Ways and Means Committee held windfall-tax hearings. According to Robert M. Brandon, director of the Ralph Nader-connected Tax Reform Research Group, the committee's actions were "a sham." *The New York Times* backed up Brandon's analysis. It was doubtful, said the *Times,* if the oil companies would be paying any more taxes than they had in the past: which meant virtually none.

The big oil companies are controlled by a tiny number of men. None of them, however, are dominated so completely by one family as is massive Gulf Oil by the Mellons of Pittsburgh and, in particular, by one Mellon: Paul. Like its other Sisters, Gulf pays very little in federal income taxes: 0.81 percent of net income in 1968; 0.43 percent in 1969; and 1.2 percent in 1970.

Gulf and its Sisters enriched themselves handsomely from the energy crisis. Exxon had a 59 percent profit increase over the fourth quarter of 1972 during the fourth quarter of 1973; Mobil's increase was 68 percent; Shell's was 55 percent; Texaco's was 70 percent. Ahead of them all was Gulf at 91 percent.

The energy crisis began to disappear like magic when the Seven Sisters got what they wanted: higher prices, the easing of environmental standards, the Alaskan pipeline, and elimination of competition from independents.

In one master stroke the Sisters pulled off a coup worth billions. Seven companies, for their own enrichment, brought economic hardship to entire nations. How could such power be concentrated in so few hands? A look at the Mellons of Pittsburgh—Thomas Mellon, his son Andrew, and his grandson Paul—will provide many of the answers. So too will a look at the Mellon empire.

What an empire it is! There are interests in hundreds of companies, but especially there are the five glittering diamonds in the corporate crown. One of those diamonds is Gulf Oil, which Paul Mellon literally owns, whose subsidiaries at the end of 1972 included: Gulf Refining Co.; Transocean Gulf Oil Co.; Colombian Gulf Oil Co.; Gulf Exploration Co.; Gulf Kuwait Co.; Gulf Iran Co.; Gulf International Co.; Mene Grande Oil Co.; Venezuela Gulf Refining Co.; Propet Co., Ltd. (Bahamas); Bolivian Gulf Oil Co.; Afran Bahamas Ltd.; Cabinda Gulf Oil Co.; Afran Transport Co. (Liberia); Caribbean Gulf Refining Corp.; Gulf Petroleum, S. A. (Panama); China Gulf Plastics Corp.; Singapore Gulf Plastics, Ltd.; Pacific Gulf Oil, Ltd.; Petroleo Gulf de Guatemala, S. A.; Ecuadorian Gulf Oil Co.; Gulf Oil Export Co.; Gulf Plastic Products Co.; Gulf Sekiyu Seisel Co., Ltd. (Ryukyu Islands); Sequoia Refining Corp.; Gulftankers, Inc. (Liberia); Toronto Pipe Line Co. (Del.); Okan Pipeline Co.; West Texas Gulf Pipe Line Co.; Gulf Italiana S.p.A. (Italy); Gulf Oil A/S (Denmark); Gulf Benzin A/S; Gulf Oil Refining A/S; Gulf Oil (Belgium) S.A.; Belgulf Tankers, S.A.; Gulf Oil (Luxembourg) S.A.; Gulf Oil (Switzerland); Gulf Europe Co. (Liechtenstein); Gulf Research and Development Co.; Gulf Oil Co. (Nigeria), Ltd.; Gulf Oil Canada, Ltd.; Gulf Oil Co. of Pennsylvania; Gulf Oil Deutschland, G.m.b.H.; Gulf Oil (G.B.), Ltd.; Britama Tankers Ltd.; Gulf Oil (India), Ltd.; Gulf Oil Refining Ltd.; Gulf Oil Terminals (Ireland), Ltd.; Gulf Oil (Nederland) N. V.; Frisia Mineralolien N. V.; Gulf Oil Raffinaderij (Gulf Oil Refining) N. V.; Gulf Research Laboratoria N. V.; Nedgulf Tankers N. V.; Sociedad Anonima Espanola de Lubrificantes; Compania Maritima Rio Gulf, S. A.; Dominion Gulf Co.; Gulf Oil Trading Co.; Kupan International Co. (Liberia); Gulf Asian Services, Inc. (Liberia) ; Gulf Asian Terminals, Inc. (Liberia); Pittsburgh and Midway Coal Mining Co.; Nigerian Gulf Oil Co.; Gulf Oil Germany, Inc.; Erdoelwerke Frisia A. G.; Frisia Handels und Transport G.m.b.H.; Gulf Deutschland G.m.b.H.; Frisia Mineralol S.A.R.L.; Svenska Gulf Oil Co. A. B.; Blackships, Inc.; Bulk Petroleum Corp.; and Tremarco Corp.

But Gulf is bigger still. Here are Gulf's affiliates, and therefore in a real sense, Paul Mellon's affiliates, with the company's percentage of ownership:

United Petroleum Securities Corp. (22.5); Four Corners Pipe Line Co. (20); Korea Oil Corp. (50); Laurel Pipe Line Co. (40); Colonial Pipeline Co. (14.9); Chinhae Chemical Co., Ltd. (50); Kuwait Oil Co., Ltd. (50); Kuwait Chemical Fertilizer Co. (20); Cherokee Pipe Line Co. (50); Explorer Pipe Line Co. (20.8); A-Jin Chemical Co., Ltd. (50); Heung Kuk Sang Sa Co., Ltd. (50); Dixie

Pipeline Co. (18.2); Oil Shippers Service (20); Palomaco (20); Mathews Phillips (49); Venture Out in America, Inc. (49); Greenland Oil Co. (25); Petroleum Products Storage & Transport Co. (50); Svensk Petroleumforvalting A.B. (22.7); Pan-Eastern Refining Co., Ltd. (50); Compania Yacibol Bogoc Transportadores (50); Berry Wiggins & Co., Ltd. (26.5); Haroon Oils, Ltd. (30); Fertilizantes de Iberia S.A. (50); Refineria de Petroleos del Norte S.A. (40.5); Rio Gulf Commercial S.A. (50); Rio Gulf de Petroleos S.A. (40); Rio Gulf Petrolquimica S.A. (50); Raffinerie de Cressier S.A. (25); Delaware Bay Transportation Co. (33.3); General Facilities, Inc. (50); Iowa Oil Company (33.3); Allied Gulf Nuclear Services (50); Korea Lubricants Co., Ltd. (50); Korea Oil Corp. (50); Gulf Disney Enterprises [California] (50); Gulf Disney Enterprises [Florida] (50).

By the end of 1970 Gulf had assets of $8,672,298,000. How much of this did Paul and other Mellon family members control?

Between 1937 and 1939 the Temporary National Economic Committee (TNEC) investigated how stock was owned among 1,710 major corporations. It was the last time the American public was treated to an inside look at the holdings of the very rich. The TNEC study revealed that the Mellon family owned a phenomenal 70.24 percent of Gulf's common stock. In *The Rich and the Super-Rich*, Ferdinand Lundberg calculated what that 70.24 percent would have been worth at closing 1964 prices: $4,254,972,426. A good portion of that would belong to Paul Mellon, Andrew Mellon's only son; a good enough portion, in fact, that Paul could have called the shots at Gulf.

Today Lundberg's calculation of the Mellon holdings

in Gulf would be extremely low. The company's assets in 1964 were $4,667,070,000. By 1972 that figure had more than doubled.

Regardless, the Mellon power derived from more than just Gulf Oil. The second of their five precious diamonds is the Aluminum Company of America, with the following subsidiaries at the end of 1972: Alcoa Building Products, Inc.; Alcoa Exploration Company; Companhia De Mineracao Santarem-Comisa (Brazil); Canada, Ltd.; Alcoa International, Inc. (Panama); Alcoa Finance Corporation; Alcoa Marine, Inc.; Australasian Minerals; H. C. Products Co.; Indonesian Minerals, Inc.; L. W. Nash Co.; Ocean Search, Inc.; P. T. Alcoa Minerals of Indonesia; Yadkin, Inc.; Alcoa de Centro America, S. A.; Alcoa Fuels, Inc.; Alcoa Inter-America, Inc.; Alcoa Deutschland G.m.b.H.; Alcoa International Canada, Ltd.; Alcoa International, Inc. (Panama) ; Alcoa International (Asia), Ltd.; Alcoa France S.A.R.L.; Alcoa Minerals of Jamaica; Alcoa of Australia, Ltd.; Alcoa of Australia (W.A.), Ltd.; Alcoa Holdings, Ltd.; Dowell Australia, Ltd.; Alcoa Generating Corp.; Alcoa of Costa Rica; Alcoa Sport Products; American Powdered Metals Co.; Moralco, Ltd. (Japan); N. W. Alloys, Inc.; Lot 8, Inc.; Alcoa Properties, Inc.; Washington Plaza Development, Inc.; Washington Plaza, Inc.; Century Malibu, Inc.; Alcoa Ventures, Inc.; ARI Staten, Inc.; Challenge Developments, Inc.; Century City, Inc.; Allegheny Center Associates; Alcoa Towers, Inc.; Alcoa Florida, Inc.; Alcoa Construction Systems, Inc.; Alcoa Securities Corp.; Alcoa Cutlery Corp.; Alcoa Service Corp.; Alcoa Steamship Co.; Aluminio Alcoa (Venezuela) S. A.; Inversiones Araco Compania Anonima; ACO, Sociedad Anonima; Alcomex, S. A. (Mexico); Adam Metal Supply, Inc.; Adam Metal Supply of Long Island; Adam Metal Supply

12

of New Jersey; Alcoa (Nederland) N. V.; Tifton Aluminum Company; Badin Water Co.; Bauxite & Northern Railway Co.; Alcoa of Great Britain, Ltd.; Alcoa Container Systems (G. B.), Ltd.; Alcoa Foils (G.B.), Ltd.; Alcoa Manufacturing (G.B.), Ltd.; Almin Patents, Ltd.; Bayswater Tubes and Sections, Ltd.; International Alloys, Ltd.; Long Sault, Inc.; Rea Magnet Wire Co., Inc.; Cedar Rapids Transmission Co., Ltd.; Colockum Transmission Co.; Lavaca Pipe Line Co.; Lavaca Production Co.; Lib-Ore Steamship Co. (Liberia); Norsk Alcoa A/S; Massena Terminal Railroad Co.; Nantahala Power and Light Co.; Point Comfort Water Co.; Point Comfort & Northern Railway Co.; Rockdale, Sandow & Southern Railroad Co.; Suriname Aluminum Co.; Tapoco, Inc.; Victoria Aluminum Co.; and Wear-Ever Aluminum, Inc.

Alcoa's major affiliates are: Aluminio, S. A. de C. V. (Mexico); Furukawa Aluminum Co. Ltd. (Japan); Halco (Mining) Inc.; and Lips Aluminum B. V. (Netherlands).

Big Aluminum, the Number One producer in the world of an indispensable metal, and Paul could have run the company for the asking. The TNEC study of 1937–1939 revealed that the Mellon family owned 33 percent of Alcoa's common stock, and Lundberg estimates that 33 percent would have been worth $438,970,087 in 1964. Again, however, Lundberg's figure would be extremely low today, since Alcoa's assets have almost doubled since he made his calculations. In any case, for Paul Mellon there was still more, there was the third gem in the five-tipped crown: Koppers, and its subsidiaries and affiliates (as of the end of 1972):

Koppers Products, Ltd.; Koppers of Canada, Ltd.; Koppers Interamerican Co.; Koppers Interamerican Sales Co.; Koppers International (Australia); Ltd.; Koppers de Mexico S. A.; Koppers de Venezuela C. A.; U. S.

Plastic & Chemical Corp.; Koppers World Trade Corp.; Andrew Brown Co.; Buffalo Slag Co.; Buffalo Gravel Corp.; Erie Sand & Gravel Corp.; Erie Sand Steamship Co.; Ontario-Lake Erie Sand, Ltd.; Arcade Blacktopping Service; International Consulting Services; Susquehanna Quarry Co.; Koppers Comercio é Servicos Technicos, Ltda.; Koppers International C. A. (Venezuela); Koppers of Turkey, Inc.; Koppers of Liberia, Inc.; Eastern Rock Products, Inc.; Gen. Crushed Stone Co.; Chester Carriers, Inc.; Easton Mack Truck Sales, Inc.; Stone Man, Inc.; Kentucky Stone Co.; Gorman Construction Co.; Koppers Far East; Koppers Sales Co.; Sinclair-Koppers Co.; Sinclair-Koppers Chemical Co.; Sinclair-Koppers International, Inc.; Lycoming Silica Sand Co.; Swanson Lumber Co., Ltd.; TPL Industries, Ltd.; Teepee Pole & Piling, Ltd.; Amfab Products, Ltd.; Universal Corrugated Box Machinery Corp. A. G.; Universal Corrugated Box Machinery Corp., G.m.b.H.; Universal Corrugated Box Machinery Corp. (Holland); Impregnadores de Maderas de Guatemala S. A.

Affiliates include: American Aniline Products, Inc.; Koppers Australia Pty. Ltd.; Koppers-Hickson Canada, Ltd.; Koppers-Hickson (Chile); Railway Tie Corp. of America; Maderas del Norte S. A.; Ingenieria y Construccion Sigdo Koppers S. A.; Eickhoff-Universal Wellpappenmaschinen G.m.b.H.; and Isowa-Hooperswift, Ltd.

Koppers, which is incorporated in Delaware because of that state's lenient tax laws, manufactures scores of products, including tar, asphalt, piston rings, railroad ties, utility poles, coke ovens, and blast furnaces. Koppers had 215 plants and assets at the end of 1972 of $470,784,-000. The 1937–1939 TNEC Study revealed that the Mellons owned 52.5 percent of Koppers' common stock, which Lundberg calculated was worth $64,599,968 in 1964. However, since 1964 the company's assets have increased more than $250 million.

The fourth gem in the Mellon corporate crown is Carborundum, with the following affiliates and subsidiaries, as of the end of 1972: R. C. Bowers Supply Co.; Barthmann Cristall G.m.b.H. (West Germany); Carborundum (Far East), Ltd.; Electro Metalurgia Abrasivos Salto S. A. (Brazil); Torrax Systems, Inc.; Canadian Carborundum, Ltd; Lockport-Warwick Felts, Ltd.; Lockport Felt, Ltd.; Spode (Canada), Ltd.; Canada Sand Papers, Ltd.; Carborundum Overseas Corp.; Carborundum (New Zealand), Ltd.; Carborundum International S. A. (Switzerland); Carborundum Co. of Puerto Rico; Carborundum Belgium S.A./N.V.; Carborundum France S.A.; Carborundum Italia S.p.A.; Carborundum-Nederland N.V.; Carboscan A/S; Carborundum Caribbean, Inc.; Spode, Inc.; Commercial Filters Canada, Ltd.; Carborundum Co., Ltd. (G. B.); Pollett Brothers, Ltd.; F. E. Rowland & Co., Ltd.; W. T. Copeland & Sons, Ltd.; Mitchell Grinding Wheel Co., Ltd.; Spencer & Halstead, Ltd.; Hepburn Conveyor Company, Ltd.; Williams & Womersley, Ltd.; Cash Management, Ltd.; Jonas Wells, Ltd.; Hammersley & Co., Ltd.; United Abrasives, Ltd.; United Carborundum Works, Ltd.; Spode, Ltd.; Vincit Carriers, Ltd.; Union Glue & Gelatin Co., Ltd.; Carborundum Proprietary, Ltd.; John Oakey & Sons (Australia) Proprietary, Ltd.; Pangborn Canada, Ltd.; Torrax Services, Ltd.; Carborundum Intl. Sales Corp.; Carborundum Intl. C. A. (Venezuela); Esmeriles Nacionales C. A. (Venezuela); Abrasivos, C. A. (Venezuela); A/S Arendal Smelteverk (Norway); Carborundum-Werke G.m.b.H. (West Germany); C. F. Schroder Schmirgelwerke (West Germany); Pangborn

Europe S.p.A. (Italy); A/S Carboscan/Carborundum (Denmark); Carborundum Industrias Abrasivas (Spain); Carborundum S. A. (Brazil); Carborundum S. A. Industrial y Commercial (Argentina); Carborundum-Universal, Ltd. (Zambia). Affiliates are: Japan Pur. Co. Ltd. (Japan); Toshiba Monofrax Co., Ltd. (Japan); Carborundum Universal, Ltd. (India); Universal Carborundum Australia Proprietary, Ltd.; Compania Nacional de Abrasivos S.A. (Mexico); Fabrica Nacional de Lija, S. A. de C. V. (Mexico); Nippon Coated Abrasive Co., Ltd.; Nippon Kynol K.k.L. (Japan); and Nihon Ekonol K. K. (Japan).

Carborundum, with fifty-eight plants and assets through 1972 of $298,616,000, manufactures garbage disposal systems, refrigeration and air-conditioning circuits, china and crystal ware, aircraft armor, silicon carbide for guided missiles, and special borides and nitrides for the nuclear power industry, to name just a few of its products. *Fortune* magazine, October 1967, placed Mellon ownership of Carborundum at a solid 20 percent of outstanding shares.

The fifth gem in the corporate crown is the Mellon National Bank & Trust Company, the largest bank in Pennsylvania with ninety-five branches, and one of the fifteen largest in the United States. The TNEC study did not delve into the ownership of the Mellon Bank, but if it had it would have revealed that Mellon ownership is as complete as it is in Gulf Oil. The bank's forerunner—T. Mellon & Sons—was opened for business by Paul's grandfather in 1869 and it has remained a family company ever since.

Federal law prevents a bank from directly owning other companies, but Mellon National, through stock it holds in its combined trust departments—stock which it votes—controls dozens of other corporations. At the end of 1972, Mellon National Bank & Trust had assets of $7,404,693,000.

Gulf, Alcoa, Koppers, Carborundum, and the Mellon National Bank were the Big Five Andrew Mellon would turn over to Paul, but the TNEC Study revealed there were substantial holdings in a variety of other companies: Allis-Chalmers Manufacturing Co.; Bethlehem Steel Corp.; Jones & Laughlin Steel Corp.; General American Transportation Corp.; Lone Star Gas Corp.; Niagara-Hudson Power Corp.; Pittsburgh Coal Co.; Pittsburgh Plate Glass Co.; The Virginian Railway Co.; Westinghouse Electric and Manufacturing Co.; and others.

What Paul Mellon inherited may have been the largest fortune ever passed from father to son. Just one of the companies, Gulf Oil, along with Gulf's six Sisters, could bring panic to such industrial domains as rubber, plastics, textiles, automobiles, coal, steel, livestock feed, and numerous others. The energy crisis dipped into almost every area of modern life, and although it abated a bit when the oil companies got their way the possibility was quite real that it could be brought back at the whim of the oil magnates, whenever it suited their purposes.

Although Paul Mellon controlled Gulf Oil and profited from the company's wheeling and dealing, he found business distasteful and let others run the family enterprises. In fact, as a man of culture and patron of the arts, he did not care to dwell on how the vast family fortune had been made.

Two

PAUL MELLON'S GRANDFATHER, THOMAS, WAS BORN ON February 3, 1813, in Camp Hill, County Tyrone, Northern Ireland, and he crossed the Atlantic Ocean with his parents, Andrew and Rebecca Wauchob Mellon, when he was five. The family settled on a farm in an area of western Pennsylvania aptly named Poverty Point. Thomas Mellon's parents were poor, God-fearing Presbyterians, but not all of their religious zeal rubbed off on their son. A different savior would rescue him from Poverty Point, and its name was *Money*.

Thomas Mellon was nine years old when he made his first journey to Pittsburgh, twenty-one miles distant, and he traveled alone, walking the whole way. One of the first sights he saw was the vast farmstead of the Negleys, wealthy Pennsylvanians, and he never forgot: "The whole scene was new to me. I remember wondering how it could be possible to accumulate such wealth, and how magnificent must be the style of living and what pleasures they must enjoy who possessed it. I remember also of the thought occurring whether I might one day attain

18

in some degree such wealth, and an equality with such great people."

Thomas Mellon could not have known that one day he would marry a Negley and that she would give birth to the shrewdest and perhaps the richest American businessman of all time. But he never forgot that first trip to Pittsburgh, nor did he ever lose sight of his ambition to reach "equality with such great people."

It seemed an unlikely dream. At age twelve Thomas Mellon was working from dawn to dusk in his father's fields and tending the family still on the side. He was also reading everything he could get his hands on, especially *Poor Richard's Almanac,* of which he later wrote in his autobiography: "Here was Franklin, poorer than myself, who by industry, thrift, and frugality had become learned and wise, and elevated to wealth and fame. The maxims of *Poor Richard* exactly suited my sentiments."

Thomas Mellon adopted without question the Puritan Ethic. The ethic was the ideological reflection of the rise of a business aristocracy, which professed that making money was God's will. "Work is Prayer," Thomas Mellon believed.

It was an uncle, Thomas, for whom he was named, who supplied him with books and encouraged his academic inclinations. The younger Thomas Mellon became acquainted with many of the classics, though he later regretted this frivolous activity: "It is wonderful how soon the memory loses such knowledge as we do not keep in constant use; and this hint from nature's law should teach us not to waste our precious time in youth laying up treasures to be lost."

Actually, Thomas Mellon's early interest in education was typical of the time. America's middle class wanted a nation built and knowledge was essential. Great libraries were constructed—including the Library of Congress and New York City's Mercantile Library— and the works of James Fenimore Cooper and Washington Irving were widely distributed. By 1819 Walter Scott's *Ivanhoe* had sold 2.5 million copies in America, and in 1820 there were some eight thousand college graduates in the country.

Thomas Mellon was a hard worker. As a boy he also recognized the need for schooling and against his father's advice he educated himself, going mostly to itinerant teachers who roamed the countryside practicing their profession free-lance style. At age twenty-one he entered the University of Western Pennsylvania (now Pittsburgh University) where he chose to study law. He was shy, soft-spoken, retiring, almost bashful, felt distinctly uncomfortable with nearly everyone, believed most people were unmannered barbarians while he was filled with culture, and at first had hesitated to take up law because he feared having to make impassioned, unseemly orations in court. Later he discovered his fears had been unfounded, as he explained in his 1885 autobiography, *Thomas Mellon and His Times*: "I was not aware then that the moneymaking part of the business lay in the background, and not in the line of speechmaking to any great extent; and that those growing rich in the profession were seldom seen in court."

Thomas Mellon met expenses at the University of Western Pennsylvania by teaching Latin during the summer (he had taught himself), helping on his father's farm, selling books door-to-door (he was a flop because he was too shy), and worked in the county clerk's office studying liens, judgments, and mortgages. The latter experience proved invaluable.

Thomas Mellon was twenty-six when he began practicing law in Pittsburgh, though a better description of what he did is loan sharking. A few of the dollars he earned in legal fees he invested, mostly in real estate, but more often he loaned his money out, taking mortgages on property as security and charging a high interest rate.

Most people in Pittsburgh in the 1840s hated entrepreneurs like Thomas Mellon. These people lived in tiny shacks, or on small farms, and they were in constant fear of losing what little they had. They had reason to fear, for the short, thin, stern-visaged Thomas Mellon was not the sort to postpone foreclosure.

Thomas Mellon accepted the Puritan Ethic. No doubt he believed in it, but it also came in handy if he was ever troubled by conscience pangs. The ethic contended that the poor were evil, that the fact they were poor proved that God looked on them with disfavor. Those who could not pay up were wastrels, gamblers or drinkers, or perhaps they sinned by going to dances. Whatever, they deserved to lose what they had.

Thomas Mellon's way of making money was foolproof. If the debtor repaid, fine, the interest Thomas Mellon reaped was quite handsome. If the debtor did not repay, however, it was even better, because Thomas Mellon was right there to foreclose on property invariably worth far more than the original loan. Meeting stiff payments on a loan was difficult in the Pittsburgh of the 1830s and 1840s, and there were many foreclosures. People were working for ten and twenty cents a day, and their children were working too. Meanwhile, in 1843, the word millionaire was coined upon the death of Pierre Lorillard, landlord, banker, and tobacconist.

Pierre Lorillard was rich, and Thomas Mellon was getting there, but for most people life was a nightmare. Many did not even have property that could be foreclosed; there were cholera outbreaks and even instances of cannibalism. Of course, there was also a surplus of cheap labor as Europeans fled the continent to escape religious persecution and war. People who did have a shack to live in, or a small farm, were being ruthlessly squeezed out by the rising business class.

What made foreclosures extra easy for Thomas Mellon was the Pennsylvania law that permitted a lender to obtain "judgment notes" and "judgment debts" from the borrower. By signing these documents the debtor waived all right even to be notified that he was losing his property. All Thomas Mellon had to do to win an immediate judgment was to go to court, which over the years he did, with startling regularity. Pittsburgh society joked that the Allegheny County sheriff was his personal employee.

Thomas Mellon stayed to himself. He had no close friends. If he was colorless and humorless, he was also untiring, a highly-determined Scotch-Irishman whose single goal in life was "to make it."

Thomas Mellon was not the world's most imaginative capitalist. He lacked vision, daring, boldness, and was too careful and conservative, unwilling to risk everything for a big financial killing. Only sure things interested him: let others go for broke was his credo; for each success he believed there were a thousand failures. "I have never seen," he wrote, "a horse race or boat race, or played a game of cards in my life, or incurred any extra hazardous risks—never speculating in property of any kind without I saw a sure thing."

Thomas Mellon may have lacked broad vision but he did possess one hallmark other fortune builders of his time had: he was seldom moved by compassion. If a man lost his home, that was too bad, but it was not his fault, he was simply honoring the letter of the law.

The Puritan Ethic even revised the Lord's Prayer to fit its need. Previously, when most wealth was property, people were asked to forgive others their "trespasses." Now they were supposed to forgive others their "debts."

Thomas Mellon could not have lived less expensively. He stayed at a rooming house and food cost two dollars a week. There were more important things to spend money on. After all, life was a business and the business of life was making money. By age thirty, after five years "practicing law," he had saved $12,000, an impressive amount in the year 1843, so he decided it was time to search for a wife. He set about the task in the same manner he looked for new investments. He was, he admitted, "compelled to extend my researches into new fields." Talking about women, he said: "Some were too gay and frivolous or self-conceited; others too slovenly and ungainly, and others again too coarse or stupid. It was a rather more difficult task than I had expected, and I was impatient of spending much time on it."

Try as he did, a suitable bride was hard to find: "It was becoming monotonous. I had now been in search of a wife for nearly six months and had spent much valuable time, somewhat to the prejudice of my professional business."

Thomas Mellon's plight is unlikely to evoke much sympathy from modern women, but the truth is that in those days a wife was as much an investment for a rising businessman as anything else. Women had few if any rights; they were quite literally their husbands' property. Their job was to raise children, to be "helpmates."

Although he claimed "a radical reform is needed in

the art of courtship," Thomas Mellon was reluctant to give up the search. He wanted someone to take care of a home for him and to save him the inconvenience of living in a rooming house and eating cold meals. Earlier he had been to the old Negley mansion to court Sarah Jane, whose family owned the estate he had admired years before on that first trip to Pittsburgh, but his efforts came to naught. The person who initially introduced him to Sarah Jane Negley was Sarah Liggett, whom he had already rejected as a marriage partner. Miss Liggett was the "right type of womanhood for wife and of a good family and very wealthy; but I feared hereditary consumption."

After striking out with Sarah Jane Negley—"I was not there to take lessons in flora culture or botany, or to learn the history of birds, fishes or butterflies. I did not want to spend evening after evening in admiring pictures in her album or in having items read to me from her scrapbook"—Thomas Mellon looked elsewhere for a bride but without success. He decided to give Sarah Jane, whom he thought "would do" as a marriage partner, another chance.

The Negleys had hit upon hard times. Roads were being built, and thousands of miles of railroads. And industry was cranking up, and the fact was that their feudal-type estate would soon become a relic of a dead age. In short, they were rich in land, but short of cash to invest in manufacturing or financing. Thomas Mellon never mentioned whether this was one of the considerations that made him think of her as a "suitable helpmate," but the truth is that later, as trustee for the family, he made handsome sums of money subdividing the property, which suddenly became valuable when Pittsburgh burst its seams and became the industrial muscle of the country.

Thomas Mellon recalled the night he proposed marriage: "There was no lovemaking and little or no love beforehand so far as I was concerned. . . . When I proposed if I had been rejected I would have left neither sad nor depressed nor greatly disappointed, only annoyed at the loss of time."

On August 22, 1843, Thomas Mellon married Sarah Jane Negley. She would give him eight children: Thomas Alexander, James Ross, Sarah Emma, Annie Rebecca, Samuel Selwyn, Andrew William, Richard Beatty, and George Negley. If history counts, by far the most important was Andrew William.

Three of the children died in childhood: Sarah Emma, Annie Rebecca, and Samuel Selwyn.

He was able to console himself over the death of his girls: "How much better may it not have been for these gentle beings to have died young: may they not have escaped a world of hardship and trouble! Females may be brought up in all the comfort and enjoyment which tender care and wealth can confer, to be launched on a hard and unfeeling world. Whilst celibacy is the safest, it has its drawbacks; and marriage is a fearful risk. Apart from the pains and anxious cares of maternity, the chances are so great of obtaining a husband who may turn out to be heartless and cruel, or a drunkard and spendthrift, and the consequences so tremendous, that daughters who die young need not be greatly lamented."

The death of his son Samuel Selwyn at age nine was an event he never got over: "Time has brought me consolation in all other deaths but this; for Selwyn I cannot be comforted."

Two other children, George Negley and James Ross, spent most of their lives plagued by poor health. George Negley finally died after a long battle with tuberculosis and although James Ross was able to conquer the same disease he was never really active in business.

Of Thomas Mellon's remaining children—all boys—only Thomas Alexander, Richard Beatty, and Andrew William grew to manhood even capable of administering what their father had begun. Although Richard Beatty would join Andrew at the bank and achieve a measure of success there, it was Andrew who made his father most proud.

While Thomas Mellon was building a family he was also building a fortune. As he watched Pittsburgh's great fire of April 10, 1845, it struck him that the building industry was about to realize boom times. He invested accordingly. Whereas earlier Thomas Mellon concentrated on personal loans secured by airtight mortgages, he more and more began to purchase real estate. This was the land the steel and coal barons would build on, and the bankers; it was land where small stores would be demolished and replaced by great factories.

On occasion Thomas Mellon could turn a 600 to 700 percent profit in a few weeks by purchasing land by the acre and then subdividing the acre into separate plots. More often, however, he held a property for months or years, eventually realizing a profit ten, twenty, thirty times what he had originally invested.

Thomas Mellon's law practice even began to flourish. Increasingly, as he was accepted by Pittsburgh's wealthy as one of their own, rich people turned to him with their legal problems. He administered their estates, invested his fees in real estate and the growing coal industry, discovered that financing small businesses in exchange for a piece of the action could bring nice profits with little work.

There was no time for sentiment. He had loaned a brother $3,000 and when the man died penniless he made the widow repay $2,000 which she had to wring from the profits of the family's small store. At the time Thomas Mellon was worth hundreds of thousands of dollars.

Thomas Mellon was cold, distant, utterly devoid of a sense of humor. He walked erect, almost excruciatingly so, and even business associates noted an "iciness" about him.

The fortune grew and grew. And his dream was the same his son Andrew would have: that his own flesh and blood would carry on what he had started. To make sure the dream became reality, Thomas Mellon decided that he would not leave the education of his children to strangers. He held a bone-deep belief that students in public schools represented a "misgoverned or neglected class of children, outcasts as it were from the parental and moral influences of a happy home. . . . Frequently coarse and low by nature, this class of schoolboy rejoices in vulgarity, disobedience, and contempt for study. Such associates are injurious to those of gentle and higher nature."

Thomas Mellon believed he was indeed of a "gentle and higher nature." The proof was his money. Like John D. Rockefeller, who said "God gave me my money," Thomas Mellon was certain that wealth proved he was one of the Almighty's chosen.

To keep his children away from "riffraff," Thomas Mellon built his own school on his own property. A few, a very few, carefully screened outsiders were admitted to defray expenses, and the school's curriculum consisted almost entirely of subjects that would produce future businessmen. "For businessmen," said the teacher at the Mellon School, "it is unnecessary to waste time on the classics and special sciences."

The teacher's remark again portrayed the ethic of the Puritan, of the God-serving Presbyterian. The Presbyterian's goal, unlike the goal of Catholics who wanted to provide at least one child who would do work for the Church, was to produce at least one businessman who would carry out the Creator's will in a different way.

Thomas Mellon closed his law office in 1859 to become a judge in the Allegheny County court of common pleas, and citizens unfortunate enough to come before him for sentencing found out what his debtors already knew: mercy did not rank at the top of a list of his virtues. Justice was meted out swiftly and sternly: "The fear of convicting and punishing an innocent party is distressing," he said. "Where innocence or guilt is made clear, however, the responsibility is light. It may seem a hard task to condemn fellow creatures to long years of confinement in a prison, or 'to be hanged by the neck until dead'; but it is not so hard if they clearly deserve it."

The people Judge Mellon sentenced were not wealthy steel and coal barons, though it could be argued that their brutal employment policies were actually causing death, but poor immigrants unable to find work to support their families. But the economy was Utopia for the businessmen: a vast supply of cheap labor and "an ever-expanding marketplace."

Judge Mellon believed in quick justice: "The manly criminal whose guilt is clear, can have no valid objection to a speedy infliction of the penalty of his crime. . . . It is this spirit perhaps to some extent which of late produces a growing tendency to self destruction on the part of criminals, and it is a course not to be discouraged. . . . Such criminals manfully rid the world of their presence, and society of the expense and trouble of their trial and punishment. It is only the mean spirited and cowardly, for the most part, who occupy the time and attention of our courts through long trials under trumped up pleas of insanity and other excuses, and invoke public sympathy to screen them from their just deserts."

Judge Mellon did not believe large court rooms were desirable. "About forty square feet would. . . best serve the purpose of justice. The general public have no necessary occasion to be there. There is no need for lobby space for loafers and hangers-on."

From 1859 on Thomas Mellon was known as Judge Mellon. He reveled in the title. Even after he quit the bench he roamed Pittsburgh streets in his judicial robes.

Judge Mellon was not overwhelmed by the patriotism some people experienced during the Civil War. When his son James Ross, who was living in Milwaukee, confided that he was thinking of enlisting in the Union Army, Judge Mellon rushed off a telegram: "DON'T DO IT. I HAVE WRITTEN."

Judge Mellon followed the telegram with a letter: "It is not so much the danger as disease and idleness and vicious habits. . . . It makes me sad to see this piece of folly. . . . I had hoped my boy was going to make a smart, intelligent businessman and was not such a goose as to be seduced from his duty by the declamations of buncombed speeches."

Judge Mellon gave other reasons for staying out of the war: "It is only greenhorns who enlist. . . . Those who are able to pay for substitutes, do so, and no discredit attaches. In time you will come to understand and believe that a man may be a patriot without risking his own life or sacrificing his health. There are plenty of other lives less valuable or others ready to serve for the love of serving."

Judge Mellon explained to James Ross that hoarding money—or even simply sitting tight—was not a wise course of action during a war. "If a dollar is but a dollar when the war is over," he wrote in one of his letters, "the more we have of them, as you say, the better for us. I might keep my money at interest and lift it and put at interest again five or six times during the war and have made no more out of it and be no better off at the end of the war than in ordinary times. . . whereas if I had invested it in property of any kind and sold while prices were going up, I might have doubled it."

In the end, James Ross saw the light and sat out the war. He was merely doing what future Mellons did: making money while others were giving their "less valuable" lives. James Ross became a currency speculator during the Civil War.

None of Judge Mellon's children took part in the war against slavery. While people died at Gettysburg, Bull Run, Antietam, Vicksburg, Harpers Ferry, Fredericksburg, and Shiloh, the Mellons were making money in Pittsburgh.

Thomas Mellon resigned as a judge in December, 1869, but his years on the bench would be remembered. Judge Josiah Cohen later recalled the time when, as a young lawyer, he had appeared before Judge Mellon.

"What did you say that petition is for?" asked Judge Mellon, who had not been paying particular attention to the argument.

"For a charter, Your Honor, for a Jewish burial ground."

"A place to bury Jews?"

"Yes, sir."

"With pleasure, with pleasure."

In late December, 1869, Judge Mellon started the private banking firm of T. Mellon & Sons at 512 and 514 Smithfield Street in Pittsburgh, the site of which is now the Henry W. Oliver Building that faces Mellon Square. *Fortune* magazine, October, 1967, described why Judge Mellon had made an excellent move: "Although tardy, the Judge was in good season to catch the best part of the post-Civil War boom. Capital was in demand: a lender could get 12 percent for his money. It was a time, the Judge was to reflect later, 'when it was easy to grow rich. One had only to buy anything and wait, to sell at a profit.' "

T. Mellon & Sons prospered for a time, then came the crash of 1873, the nation's worst in fifty years. It was precipitated by the failure of Jay Cooke & Company, a banking house involved in financing the Northern Pacific Railroad, and more than five thousand businesses were ruined in the depression that followed. It was, according to Henry Clay Frick's biographer, George Harvey, "a veritable paralysis."

Banks closed by the dozens as panicked depositors scrambled over one another to withdraw their savings. At one point Judge Mellon's bank had $600,000 in deposits and only $60,000 cash. Most of the deposits had been invested in railroad bonds and in mortgages.

The bank survived. Although without personal friends, Judge Mellon was considered the very model of what a banker should be: hard-working, conscientious, conservative, honest. Even though rich customers knew about the bank's financial troubles, they stayed with Judge Mellon and the firm survived. Many depositors, however, were simply unaware of the danger the bank was in. These people, Judge Mellon observed, had not "the slightest apprehension of our solvency as I was always looked on as impregnable."

After the bust came boom, at least for the bankers, and Judge Mellon was in his glory. Although the banks were once again solvent, most people were not, and there was an orgy of foreclosures. Luckless homeowners saw their properties put up for sale by the sheriff, saw Judge Mellon gobble them up for a fraction of their value. Small businessmen lost everything. Some of these businessmen had stayed with Judge Mellon when he himself had been in danger of bankruptcy.

People starved in the streets of Pittsburgh. Families were without a roof over their heads. Strikes, which began when the Baltimore and Ohio Railroad cut wages, spread across the country. There was violence in Baltimore, Chicago, and St. Louis. President Rutherford B. Hayes called out troops. In the dog days of 1877 rioting broke out in Pittsburgh. The Pittsburgh militia refused to kill its own neighbors so soldiers were brought in from Philadelphia. They fired into an unarmed crowd and twenty persons died.

The rioting became worse. Predictably, Judge Mellon sided with those who were cutting wages. He continued to foreclose on property and stated that the trouble was caused by "the vicious classes."

"The public be damned," said William H. Vanderbilt, and Thomas Mellon agreed. The workers who huddled in Pittsburgh shacks were "subhuman," their poverty proved that God rejected them.

When the depression ended in 1880, Judge Mellon was a multimillionaire. He was rich in both cash and real estate. It was time, he reasoned, to retire. His sons, especially Andrew, were perfectly capable of building upon what he had begun.

Judge Mellon became a philosopher. He began to write his autobiography, into which he poured the wisdom he had garnered through the years. One issue he thought himself particularly expert on was Ireland. The agitation of the Irish under British rule was so intense, he said, that "the English Government was driven to measures for their expatriation or extermination. And if we compare the conditions of these northern counties and their Protestant population today, with the southern or Celtic part of Ireland, it is very manifest that it would have been well for Ireland, and well for Great Britain, had this policy of expatriation been carried into effect throughout the entire island."

Judge Mellon felt that "Ireland. . . was duly surrendered to England over seven hundred years ago. . . on the ground of their incapacity for self-government. And this incapacity has been abundantly manifested ever since."

It was clear, said Judge Mellon, that "The document [the 1155 Papal Bull of Adrian IV permitting Henry II to occupy Ireland with troops in the cause of ecclesiastical reform] is in the nature of a perpetual lease."

Although Judge Mellon had been born in Ireland, he considered himself British. He also considered Ireland British: "If we look into the Irish clamor about English usurpation and oppression, we find there is nothing in it. The British Government has as perfect a right to Ireland as to any other of her possessions—as much as to the soil of England itself."

Judge Mellon never tired of talking about Ireland. He even saw a similarity between American Indians and the Irish: "The lower the scale of humanity, the more unreasoning and more violent the passions for good or evil. Of course where hate, fear, jealousy and revenge are in constant exercise, these malevolent passions are the most developed, and predominate. We find precisely the same conditions resulting from the same causes among our North American Indian tribes. . . and wherever else the savage state exists: producing a sparsity of population and a state of degradation approaching the nature of the predatory animal. . . . Their (the Irish) improvement by connection with England has been exceedingly slow."

The older Judge Mellon grew, the more fanatic he became about Ireland, "the land of my birth and that of my immediate ancestors." He said that "England's policy toward the Irish, it is true, has been unwise and unfortunate. But its unwisdom has been on the side of too great leniency and toleration." Speaking of Cromwell, who murdered hundreds of thousands of Irish, Judge Mellon said he "was the only ruler who understood their nature, and governed them accordingly." Finally, Judge Mellon offered a solution to the whole mess: "It certainly would be a blessing to the Irish themselves, if by some social force they could be scattered over all the earth, and not a vestige of them left on their own soil."

Judge Mellon considered himself an authority on genealogy. At first he claimed the "Mellon" name was "so ancient as to be prehistoric," but later he said, "The name Mellon. . . originated among the Greeks, where, in the Theban dialect, it meant 'future hope'. . . and according to the meaning of our name, therefore, every young Mellon may be truthfully regarded as a 'young hopeful.' "

Judge Mellon had ideas on many subjects. For example, crime: "Murder, robbery, and violence of every degree of atrocity, and fraud, embezzlement and dishonesty have become so common as to attract little attention."

On organized crime: "These dangerous criminals. . . the unions. . ." consist of "mobs of striking miners" armed with "repeating rifles" and "drilling under anarchist leaders."

On rascally lawyers: "There is no greater danger a client can encounter than to fall into the hands of one of these supercilious pretenders; he is sure to be fleeced unmercifully, regardless of any professional benefits conferred. . . . Where the fee is obtained without an equivalent in benefits conferred, the goose is killed that laid the golden egg: for the goose that once pays such a fee is not likely to pay another to the same attorney, and is apt to warn off the rest of the flock."

On socialism: It "is the desire of him who has nothing, to share with him who has; the desire of the idler, the worthless and good for nothing, to place himself on a footing of equality with the careful, industrious, and thrifty."

On education: "Read no frivolous works like novel reading and light literature—it unhinges the mind entirely for manly employment."

Judge Mellon's portrait still hangs in the board room of the Mellon National Bank & Trust Company, mute tribute to the corporate empire he started. But it is his son's portrait that really should hang there. Even thrifty old Judge Mellon, who died on his ninety-fifth birthday, February 3, 1908, would agree.

Three

PAUL MELLON'S FATHER, ANDREW, WAS BORN ON MARCH 24, 1855, attended the University of Western Pennsylvania for a little more than two years, then at age eighteen began running a lumber business in Mansfield, eight miles from Pittsburgh, which Judge Mellon had bought for him. He stayed with the business for a little more than a year, wisely sold out for a profit just before the 1873 crash, and joined T. Mellon & Sons. No man who ever lived was better suited for banking. "Andrew Mellon," said *Fortune* magazine in 1967, "was possibly the most brilliant businessman whom our society has produced."

Andrew Mellon resembled his father a good deal physically. He was thin, with a hawk's face, five feet, nine inches tall, and he seldom smiled, never laughed. He had grey-blue eyes, like Judge Mellon he was ramrod straight, and his shy, reserved manner belied perhaps the boldest and most inventive business mind in the world. "Stern," was the way associates described him.

Andrew Mellon was indeed his father's son. As a little

boy he had often crouched under his father's bench, unnoticed, listening as his father doled out justice. When he grew up he was not the sort people approached on the sidewalk and engaged in conversation. His facial expression, which seldom changed, was almost forbidding, and he was nearly always in a hurry. "When you saw him coming," said an officer of T. Mellon & Sons, "you were wise to get out of his way."

Andrew Mellon met steel magnate Henry Frick in 1877, and they remained friends and associates until Frick died in 1919. When Frick made his first million at the age of thirty in 1879, Andrew Mellon and he celebrated the event with a trip to Europe. They visited Ireland, England, France,. Austria. Andrew Mellon became interested in art, a hobby he pursued with a passion just slightly less heated than his pursuit of wealth. Already he was envisioning financial vistas his provincial father was incapable of even imagining.

In 1880 Judge Mellon appointed his not yet twenty-six-year-old son as head of the bank. Andrew Mellon promptly went to work. He acquired the Pittsburgh Bank of Commerce to handle the accounts of workingmen. (T. Mellon & Sons was mainly set up to do business with industry.) In 1883 Andrew Mellon expanded again, buying the Union Insurance Company. He saw no reason why Mellon-owned companies should pay insurance premiums to companies they did not own.

The year 1889 was an important one for Andrew Mellon. Two metallurgists—Alfred Hunt and George Clapp —came to him with a new process for smelting aluminum. The idea looked good to the thirty-four-year-old banker and he provided $250,000 in credit to get the enterprise underway. He provided the credit in exchange for control of the company, the Pittsburgh Reduction

Company, now the huge Aluminum Company of America.

Andrew Mellon did not invent the idea of loaning money in exchange for control of a business. That had first been done by New York bankers. What Andrew Mellon did was copy the idea, copy it so effectively in fact that even Wall Street would weep with envy.

In 1889 Andrew Mellon formed another company, a bank, the Union Transfer & Trust Company, soon renamed Union Trust. The plan was for the bank to move into the trust business—handling estates, investing the money of wealthy inheritors—in a big way. People were either very rich or very poor in Pittsburgh, and Union Trust began as a bank for the very rich.

Andrew Mellon was assisted at the bank by his brother Richard Beatty, the only other son of Judge Mellon who could truly be labeled a success in business. Richard Beatty could best be described as a playboy, a hail-fellow-well-met. He enjoyed playing polo and hunting foxes and was one of the most prominent figures in Pittsburgh social circles. It was Richard Beatty, open, cheerful, blustery, who met the public Andrew Mellon disliked and shied away from. For Andrew Mellon it was enough to sit deep in the recesses of his bank and plan deals. People afraid to approach him—which meant almost everyone—went to the jovial Richard Beatty.

Andrew Mellon bought up Pittsburgh property by the block. He invested in coal, iron, steel. He was banker for the great Pittsburgh industrialists, and he was an industrialist in his own right. His money and influence extended into every nook of the city, and beyond.

One business eluded him—Westinghouse. His opportunity came in 1890 when George Westinghouse needed $500,000. Andrew Mellon agreed to loan the money, provided the bank could name the Westinghouse general manager. That would, of course, have been the first step, albeit a small one, toward a takeover. George Westinghouse recognized Andrew Mellon's offer for what it was, and went to New York City for his money.

Andrew Mellon waited patiently, like a spider in its net. He even watched with bemused interest during the crash of 1908 when the New York bankers squeezed Westinghouse out entirely. Andrew Mellon went quietly about the job of increasing his stock in Westinghouse and finally, in the depression year of 1930, moved forward to assume a role equal with Wall Street.

Andrew Mellon's friend Henry Frick was importing people from Hungary and Italy and Yugoslavia to work his coke ovens and was paying them next to nothing. He and Andrew Mellon felt there was no need to clean up the environment, which was probably the filthiest on earth. Indeed, many wealthy Pittsburghers believed that the "subhuman" immigrants probably thrived on the heat of the coal ovens and the gases they had to breathe. In fact, Andrew Mellon stated that fresh air would probably be harmful for the workers, whom rich people called "Wops" and "Polacks" and "Hunkies." The fresh air issue was a rationalization for exploitation, of course, but Andrew Mellon and Henry Frick probably really believed that fresh air was harmful for workers. If God intended workers to breathe fresh air, the reasoning went, He would not have inspired the building of industry.

Andrew Mellon was thoroughly in agreement with Frick's methods of preventing and smashing strikes which, according to Philip Foner's *History of the American Labor Movement*, included torture and beatings and murder administered by paid private police.

Henry Frick presided over one of the bloodiest strikes in American labor history. The year was 1892, the place was Homestead, Pennsylvania. The strike began when management announced a pay cut. Frick brought in a barge filled with scores of gunmen to smash the workers, who retaliated by firing on the thugs and making them captives. Then Governor Pattison called out state troopers, and they occupied Homestead for ninety-five days.

The entire country was for the Homestead strikers, but Frick refused to budge an inch. From New York came anarchist Alexander Berkmann: he stabbed and knifed Frick, but failed to kill him.

When it was announced that Frick had been wounded a soldier let out three cheers. The soldier was hung by his thumbs.

Andrew Mellon hastened to Frick's bedside and remained with his friend until he was out of danger.

The strikers lost. Ten persons died in the Homestead strike, and many more were wounded.

In 1899 Andrew Mellon conceived his grandest plan. He and Henry Frick would build the Union Steel Company and challenge mighty Andrew Carnegie. Carnegie was unimpressed. He had intended to retire anyway and sell huge Carnegie Steel. He went to New York but Wall Street did not offer enough. He went to Andrew Mellon. Why not, Carnegie suggested, go into steel in a really big way? Union Steel and Carnegie Steel would be a corporate marvel.

Andrew Mellon offered $160 million, saying he would put up $80 million and would try to raise the rest. He tried to obtain the second $80 million from J. P. Morgan, who laughed at him. The price, said Morgan, was too high.

J. P. Morgan was wrong. Within two years Morgan

was scrambling to organize the first billion-dollar company—U.S. Steel—and to succeed he needed to purchase Carnegie Steel. It cost him $492 million to do it, more than three times what Carnegie had been willing to sell it for to Andrew Mellon. And still Morgan had problems: Andrew Mellon and Henry Frick.

Mellon and Frick went about building Union Steel. The plant would be in Donora, named for tin magnate W. H. Donner, and for Nora McMullen, who married Mellon in 1900.

Andrew Mellon picked up other companies: Republic Coke; Schoen Works; Pressed Steel Car; McClintic-Marshall Construction. Nevertheless, Union Steel, renamed Union-Sharon Steel through a merger, remained Andrew Mellon's pet project. After all, he was holding his own in competition with the greatest financier of them all—J. P. Morgan. Now it was Andrew Mellon who could laugh.

Some people dislike heights. Others despise war. The thing J. P. Morgan hated above all else was competition. He considered competition wasteful and self-defeating, something only free enterprisers and fools believed in; it drove prices and profits down, led to anarchy in the marketplace.

Morgan tried to buy Union-Sharon Steel. Finally, when his offer reached $75 million, Andrew Mellon and Henry Frick accepted. It was far more than their company was worth. For example, part of the purchase price was $4,000,000 for an ore mine that had cost Union-Sharon only $150,000 several years earlier. A special House of Representatives committee that was established specifically to investigate U.S. Steel pointed out how Andrew Mellon and Henry Frick were able to get the best of the mighty Morgan:

"The aggressive attitude of the company [Union-

Sharon] and the capacity and long experience in business of Mr. Frick and others associated with him caused the Steel Corporation grave concern. The methods which had either destroyed or rendered tractable the smaller companies could not be rendered effective to eliminate the Union-Sharon Steel Company. . . . It soon became manifest that this company would not 'push.' Located in the midst of the Corporation's great plants, it was in a position to render its competition especially troublesome. . . . There remained but one solution—to pay such price as those in charge might deem for an agreement not to further disturb industrial conditions which the Steel Corporation sought to establish, or compete with them for the business. The Corporation decided to pay."

The year 1901 was probably the most important in Andrew Mellon's life, though he could not have known it at the time. On January 9 of that year a Yugoslav prospector named Anthony Luchich brought in the spectacular Spindletop Gusher, the world's biggest oil discovery up to that time. Spindletop gave almost 100,000 barrels a day. Overnight sleepy little Beaumont, Texas, twenty miles away, was a boom town.

The oil was there, but how was Luchich to bring it to a market? He received some money from Guffey and Gale, Pittsburgh oil speculators, but soon they too were short of cash. Guffey went to the Mellon bank and received a sympathetic hearing. Before long a deal was made: the J. M. Guffey Petroleum Company would take over Spindletop; prospector Luchich was bought out for $400,000; Guffey was handed $1 million and the company's presidency.

To assure a favorable political climate, former Texas Governor James Hogg was given a slice of the action.

Hogg had powerful friends in the Lone Star State. He also had a bizarre sense of humor. He named his daughter Ima.

The Mellons retained forty percent of the Guffey stock. The remainder was spread among six wealthy Pittsburghers and what happened is history. Guffey was soon squeezed out, the Mellons bought up most of the stock they had originally sold, and lucrative Gulf Oil was born. Andrew Mellon, who never spent a day of his life in an oil field, would leave a company powerful enough to challenge the Rockefellers for control of the world's most needed fuel.

There was so much to do. Andrew Mellon organized the Monongahela River Consolidated Coal & Coke company [River Coal] into a monopoly. The company owned ninety-six mines, forty-four boat companies, forty thousand acres of land, and was serviced by eighty steamboats and three thousand barges.

Andrew Mellon found time for smaller deals. In 1901 he bought five lots on Pittsburgh's Sixth Avenue for $241,000. A year later he sold them for $400,000.

In 1902 Andrew Mellon scrapped his private bank, T. Mellon & Sons, and founded the Mellon National Bank, federally chartered. The next year he merged Pittsburgh National and Citizens National with Union Trust.

It was boom one year, bust the next, around the turn of the century, but neither state of the economy affected Andrew Mellon. In boom times he counted stock dividends, interest payments, trust charges, expanded production in companies he had purchased earlier. When the economy went bust it was like Judge Mellon's heyday: foreclose; buy up property at a fraction of its value; force weaker companies to sell or merge with stronger ones.

Andrew Mellon rode horses occasionally, and played golf, but these moments of relaxation were rare and best left to Richard Beatty. For Andrew Mellon there were always new and big deals to make. Millions of dollars became hundreds of millions which in turn became a billion or more. The aluminum company, the golden black profits of oil, the real estate and industrial companies acquired at auction and by foreclosure, the soaring assets of the banks and insurance companies, all helped combine to make Andrew Mellon one of the richest men in the world.

And there was World War I. Defense contracts. Aluminum and coke and coal and oil—all were needed to keep the world safe for democracy. All could be, and were, sold to the War Department—at a profit.

Andrew Mellon spent World War I in Pittsburgh, overseeing his empire. Then, in 1920, sixty-five years old and bored after a lifetime of making money, he accepted the post of Secretary of the Treasury under newly-elected President Warren G. Harding. It was said that the reason Andrew Mellon became Treasury Secretary was a desire to receive from the general public the acclaim he had long been accorded by his peers.

When Andrew Mellon entered public office the country was split into opposing camps. America was still reeling from the Palmer Raids and was about to be traumatized by the Sacco-Vanzetti case. Workers were fighting for industrial unions, higher pay, and the eight-hour day. There were bitter, bloody strikes. Union organizers were hampered because immigrant workers spoke so many different languages, and because of the greed and shortsightedness of the upper classes.

The middle class, meanwhile, was boobish, crude, complacent. This was the same middle class that would elect three of the worst presidents in the country's history: Warren (Teapot Dome) Harding; Calvin ("The business of America is business") Coolidge; and Herbert (the 1929 Depression) Hoover.

This, then, was America in the 1920s: seething underneath, apparently prosperous and carefree on the surface.

No man appointed to public office ever had to resign from as many corporate boards as Andrew Mellon did. There were fifty-one in all, and their activities spanned the spectrum of industry and finance. Included were aluminum companies, oil companies, steel companies, companies involved in coke, coal, carbon, shipbuilding, electricity, automobiles, land development, railroads, construction, insurance, and banking.

"The government is just a business," Andrew Mellon told reporters at his first press conference. He immediately proceeded to act as though he were more interested in profits than public service. Appointing Andrew Mellon Secretary of the Treasury, observed one writer, was "like making Casanova headmaster of a school for young ladies."

Andrew Mellon became the most popular member of the Harding cabinet, at least among America's newspapers. The big papers, huge corporations themselves, hailed his every move. They had good reason to cheer.

The New York Times, a paper in which the name Andrew Mellon had never appeared prior to January 1, 1921, was ecstatic over his performance. He was lauded for reducing the public debt, but more sensible journalists like Drew Pearson, in his book *Washington Merry-Go-Round,* saw matters otherwise: "War-time expenditures would have been reduced no matter who was Secretary of the Treasury. When a nation is paying out billions of dollars to feed an army of 5,000,000 men, to buy tons of ammunition and to build fleets of ships, and when that expenditure suddenly becomes unnecessary, it requires no particular genius to bring about Treasury surpluses and tax reduction."

George Harvey in his biography of Henry Clay Frick, revealed another facet of Andrew Mellon's personality that the *Times* either did not know or did not bother to report. "It is an interesting fact, not generally known," wrote Harvey, "that the only two multi-millionaires who supported quietly, but effectively, the successful organized effort to prevent the inclusion of the U. S. in the League of Nations were Messrs. Henry Clay Frick and Andrew W. Mellon."

The enthusiastic *Times* praised Andrew W. Mellon for collecting war debts incurred by other countries. Said Drew Pearson: "The Mellon settlement of the Allied war debt was easy. Europe not only could not repay the United States what she owed for carrying on the war to end war but she needed to borrow more money with which to build up her shattered industries, construct new fleets, and maintain armies even larger than those which were ready to be mobilized when the fatal bomb struck the Archduke Franz Ferdinand at Sarajevo in 1914.

"The State Department, however, ruled that this new money could not be borrowed until the old debts had been settled. One by one, therefore, and very reluctantly, the Allies sent their delegations to Washington to receive the terms Mr. Mellon was willing to give them. On their way home, they stopped in New York and borrowed from Wall Street more than enough to pay Mr. Mellon."

In short, Andrew Mellon's collection of the war debt

funneled hundreds of millions into the coffers of his wealthy banker friends.

Andrew Mellon served for twelve years as Secretary of the Treasury, first with Harding, then with Coolidge and Hoover. The Harding and Coolidge administrations particularly might better have been called the Mellon administration. "For eight years," wrote Drew Pearson, "he dominated the national capital. For eight years his word was law with every banker throughout the land. For eight years Presidents served under him. So powerful was his influence, so great his prestige that he told them what to do and his judgment was final."

The New York Times called him "the greatest Secretary of the Treasury since Alexander Hamilton," and so he must have seemed to big business. It must have appeared to the rich, in fact, as though money were falling out of the sky into their hands. Andrew Mellon came up with the novel idea that somehow corporations had paid too much in taxes during World War I, and that these "excess" taxes should be refunded. He failed to mention that between January, 1916, and July, 1921, American corporations had reaped an after-tax profit of $38 billion. Nor did he mention that his own profits for the war years alone were estimated at $125 million.

Andrew Mellon was Santa Claus to the rich, but for other citizens his reign was a scandal. Forty corporations and individuals, including Standard Steel Car Company, Gulf Oil, and Alcoa, received tax refunds of more than $1 million each. The Hearst Star Publishing Company, a fanatic GOP cheerleader, got tax reductions of $1,737,-007 over a three-year period.

Andrew Mellon was active in other areas, if not openly, then certainly behind the scenes. In 1922 aluminum import duties were increased 250 percent by the Republican-sponsored Fordney-McCumber Tariff. In addition, the Tariff Commission lowered the import duty on linseed oil. The reason for these seemingly contradictory tariffs was clear.

Andrew Mellon had a 100 percent monopoly on American aluminum. By keeping the metal out of the country with an outrageous import duty he maintained that monopoly. The more linseed oil that came in, however, and the cheaper it got in, the better. Andrew Mellon owned two of the eight largest linseed crushers in the country.

Of all his accomplishments, one Andrew Mellon never achieved was growing old gracefully. *Who's Who,* which receives its information from the source, listed his birth date as 1852 in its 1918–1921 editions. The 1921–1929 editions contend he was born in 1854. In 1930–1931 the listing was 1855. Somehow the greatest Secretary of the Treasury since Alexander Hamilton aged only ten years in a thirteen-year span.

Still, Andrew Mellon will best be remembered for helping to reduce the taxes of rich people. Because of his recommendations, the income tax was cut from a maximum of 73 percent to 33 percent. Everyone earning more than $66,000 had their taxes cut. Everyone under that income paid the old rate. It was later discovered, to the surprise of almost no one, that the number one beneficiary of the new rate was Andrew Mellon.

In 1928 Judge Mellon's son set his sights on the highest goal of all: the presidency of the United States. He almost made it. Insiders knew that the battle between Andrew Mellon and Herbert Hoover was simply a struggle between Morgan money and Mellon money. With the help of the *New York Times,* which thought it ludicrous that such a wealthy man should *openly* run the country (Mellon was actually running it from behind the scenes), and with a powerful assist from Philadelphia machine boss William Vare, Herbert Hoover, the Morgans' man, captured the Republican presidential nomination. Such was Andrew Mellon's power, however, that after the election he remained on in Treasury.

If blame could be placed on one man for the Great Depression of 1929, that man would be Andrew Mellon. His tax reduction program put so much money into the hands of the rich that it led to an orgy of speculation that ultimately resulted in the stock market crash. The Federal Reserve Board issued numerous warnings of what was coming—warnings that were always contradicted by the Treasury Department. Andrew Mellon's optimism convinced investors that stock prices could go up forever.

So the Depression came, the greatest depression this country has ever experienced. It bothered Andrew Mellon not at all. It merely presented him with another business opportunity, a chance to swallow up weaker corporations and, when it was over, to emerge stronger than ever.

As Drew Pearson pointed out, Andrew Mellon spent his first eight years in office predicting federal deficits. This was so the government could claim it was broke and thereby deny World War I veterans their bonuses and dissuade the hard-pressed from seeking assistance. Andrew Mellon's last four years in office, however, brought predictions of surpluses, so that the Depression-plagued American public would not demand an increase in income and inheritance taxes.

When the Depression refused to fade away Andrew Mellon was like a man no longer in touch with reality. He urged people to work hard and spend money; that, he said, was the solution to the Crash. Yet how could people spend money when Andrew Mellon's banks refused to loan them any? How could they work hard when his companies laid them off and said there was no work? In May, 1931, the Secretary of the Treasury said there should be no pay cuts, but in October of the same year his Aluminum Company of America slashed wages ten percent. In June, 1932, the Aluminum Company slashed wages ten percent more.

At the Alcoa mills in New Kensington, a Pittsburgh suburb, more than half the normal work force of four thousand was laid off. A welfare worker revealed that many of those still working had been forced by the company to donate a day's pay to those who were unemployed, despite the fact that a high weekly wage for those working full-time was only twelve dollars. The aluminum company itself paid nothing to those it laid off.

Panic spread. In September, 1931, 305 banks closed. In October 522 banks closed. Some thirteen million were unemployed. National wages were 60 percent less than in 1929. U.S. industry was operating at less than half its maximum.

With Pennsylvanians starving and freezing in the streets in the winter of 1931, Governor Gifford Pinchot visited Andrew Mellon at his Washington office. Before being allowed to see the Treasury Secretary, the Governor admired the $1.7 million worth of gems Andrew Mellon had recently purchased from the Soviet Union. When the two actually sat down to talk, Governor Pinchot offered a business deal: he suggested that well-to-do Pennsylvanians lend $35 million to the state for needed relief programs; the loan would be repaid at four percent interest, as authorized by a constitutional amendment already passed, and Andrew Mellon was asked to chip in $1 million. It was a drop in the bucket for the Treasury Secretary but he refused. In his defense, so did every other rich person in Pennsylvania.

Poverty and hunger gripped the nation by its throat. Riots were commonplace. A group of World War I veterans marched on Washington and demanded the cashing of soldiers' bonus certificates. The government drove them out of Washington with armed troops under the command of Douglas MacArthur. Participating with MacArthur were Dwight Eisenhower and George Patton.

There was talk of revolution as desperate people called for desperate measures. Young Texas Representative Wright Patman (who is still in the House) was appalled by Andrew Mellon's policies and by his lack of concern for widespread suffering. Patman brought impeachment proceedings against the Treasury Secretary.

The date was January 6, 1932, a date most American newspapers seem to have forgotten: whenever Andrew Mellon's name is mentioned in print, it is as a "philanthropist" or "businessman" or "public servant." Very seldom is the word "impeachment" brought up, though that drastic course of action is precisely what was taken.

The impeachment proceedings carried the impressive title of "House Judiciary Committee Hearings on the Charges of Hon. Wright Patman Against the Secretary of Treasury," and were brought under Section 243 of Title 5 of the Code of Laws of the United States, which read as follows: "Restrictions upon Secretary of Treasury. No person appointed to the office of Secretary of Treasury, or Register, shall directly or indirectly be concerned or interested in carrying on the business of trade or commerce, or be owner in whole or in part of any sea vessel, or purchase by himself, or another in trust for him, any public lands or other public property, or be concerned in the purchase or disposal of any public securities of any State, or of the United States, or take or apply to his own use any emolument or gain for negotiating or transacting any business in the Treasury Department, other than what shall be allowed by law; and every person who offends against any of the prohibitions of this section shall be deemed guilty of a high misdemeanor and forfeit to the United States the penalty of $3,000, and forever thereafter be incapable of holding any office under the United States."

Representative Patman, to this day a thorn in the side of big banks, went on to make the rather remarkable statement that "Mr. Mellon has violated more laws, caused more human suffering and illegally acquired more property to satisfy his personal greed than any other person on earth without fear of punishment and with the sanction and approval of three chief executives of a civilized nation."

Representative Patman also revealed that Andrew Mellon, while in office, had voting stock in more than three hundred corporations engaged in "mining properties, bauxite, magnesium, carbon electrodes, aluminum, sales, railroads, Pullman cars, gas, electric light, steel railways, copper, glass, brass, steel, tar, banking, locomotives, water power, steamships, shipbuilding, oil, coke, coal, and many other different industries."

Representative Patman had a powerful case. He pointed out that Andrew Mellon:

• as Treasury Secretary was in charge of the Coast Guard, whose job was to check incoming and outgoing ships and their cargo, and that he was also in charge of customs officers, whose responsibility was to make sure that imports were properly taxed, and therefore, since he was one of the nation's largest importers and exporters he was in an obvious position to do himself favors.

• as Treasury Secretary he could and did give himself and his companies large tax rebates.

• as Treasury Secretary was *ex officio* chairman of the Federal Reserve Board, and that by law any person holding that position was forbidden to own bank stock.

• as Treasury Secretary sold liquor during Prohibition from a distillery in which he had an interest.

• as Treasury Secretary was involved in erecting public buildings, buildings which he always urged should be constructed of aluminum (his Aluminum Company was, of course, America's only producer).

Andrew Mellon did have a reply to one of Patman's charges. "I do not," he said, "hold any bank stock."

"What did you do with it?" he was asked.

"I sold it before taking office."

"To whom was it sold?"

"To my brother."

There were other questionable deals. All U.S. banks (and Andrew Mellon was chairman of the Federal Reserve Board) refused credit to the Colombian Government until it signed the Barco oil concession giving 1.5 million acres of oil land worth as much as $2 billion to Gulf Oil and a company owned largely by the Morgans. When finally the giveaway was signed, credit was miraculously available. The *New Republic* found it unfortunate that "an American Secretary of State had used his high office to persuade the National City Bank of New York to grant an unsound bank credit to the government of Colombia as a means of obtaining one of the world's largest oil concessions for a company controlled by the interests of Mr. Mellon, our Secretary of the Treasury."

Andrew Mellon contended that the National City

loan was unconnected to the granting of the Barco concession, but few people took him seriously. He was taken even less seriously when a Senate Finance Committee investigation showed that Allen Dulles, a former undersecretary of state, represented Morgan at the time; that Herbert Stabler, formerly chief of the State Department's Latin American Division, was working for Gulf; and that Andrew Mellon's former top aide, Garrard Winston, was a lawyer for National City Bank.

Representative Patman had another serious charge, and such was the wretched state of the economy and the angry mood of the populace in the 1930s that Congress was listening. Andrew Mellon was, said Patman, "more responsible for the country's poor economic condition than any other one person."

Representative Patman revealed that the War Department had paid Andrew Mellon's Koppers Company $18,-582,428.44 during World War I and that Koppers had not produced one dollar's worth of goods. Nonetheless, after the war Koppers was allowed to purchase buildings and machinery that had cost the government $2,987,200 for $600,000; and materials that cost $5,558,000 for $300,000. This second deal, it was later revealed, was made despite the fact that a different company had offered $700,000 for the materials.

The impeachment hearings proceeded without a hitch. Patman dredged up a dozen scandals. It turned out that Andrew Mellon's Standard Steel Car Company had built a plush club during World War I which was used to entertain government bureaucrats responsible for keeping war costs down. At the club all expenses—food, lodging, entertainment—were paid by Standard Steel Car. The bureaucrats were, of course, receiving expenses from the government since they were supposed to be on state business.

During the hearings Patman demonstrated that Andrew Mellon was hardly suffering because of the Depression: "The Union Trust Company is a Mellon-owned corporation in Pittsburgh. It commenced business during the panic of 1893, prospered during the panic of 1907 and the hard times of 1914, and has been paying 200 percent dividends and more during the depression years of 1930, 1931, and 1932."

Finally, Patman put the Mellon money in perspective: "The fortune I have mentioned is twice as much money as the average amount of money that has been in circulation during the past three years, or at least twice the average amount in circulation. It is twice all the gold in the United States and is equal to two-thirds of all the gold in the entire world. It is equal to one-half the value of all the property in the United States in the year 1860. It is equal to twice the value of all agricultural products sold in America by all producers during the year 1932; equal to the entire value of all property in Texas or all property in Alabama, Mississippi, and Georgia; or all property in Maryland and Virginia; or all livestock, farm implements, and machinery. It is nearly twice the expenses of the Federal Government in one year."

It is likely that Patman would have succeeded in removing Andrew Mellon from office had not President Herbert Hoover come to the rescue. He appointed Andrew Mellon ambassador to the Court of St. James. As Patman ruefully remarked, there was no way to remove from office a man who had already been removed. He called Hoover's action the equivalent of a "Presidential pardon."

If Americans were delighted to be rid of their Treasury Secretary, Europeans were happy to have him. One French newspaper analyzed his fortune and estimated that if cut into bricks of gold there would be 160,000 bricks, each with a value of a million francs. The newspaper did additional paperwork and discovered that those bricks would construct fifty-two gold houses.

Andrew Mellon became friends with royalty, threw huge parties at the embassy, was as imperious with dukes and earls as he had been with immigrant workers. But it was not to last long. Franklin Roosevelt defeated Herbert Hoover by more than seven million votes and the Republicans were swept out of office. With them went Andrew Mellon's ambassadorship.

Andrew Mellon returned to the United States to spend his last years fighting charges of corruption and income tax evasion, and trying to instill in his only male heir—Paul—a desire to become active in business. Who else was there?

There was no one, and Andrew Mellon, born not so much to wealth as to the concept of dynasty, infected at an early age with the virus of ambition, alternately pleaded with and raged at his son. Everything a young man could ask for was there, all the gold and glitter and glory. Couldn't the boy see that?

Andrew Mellon was an old man. The age had never shown before; he had been too active, too engaged. Now it came all of a sudden. The voice became weak. The cold, frightening features became pitiful. The skin grew darker, toward a death grey. Always thin, he became skeletal. At the end he could no longer even argue with Paul. He died in 1937 at the age of eighty-two.

Four

Nora McMullen, granddaughter of Peter Guinness of Irish Stout fame, married Andrew Mellon in 1900. He was forty-five then, a rock-ribbed bachelor whose only interest was the careful tending of the burgeoning fortune his father had left. Nora was a pretty, fun-loving twenty-three.

From the beginning the marriage was a disaster. The birth of a daughter, Ailsa, in 1901, and a son, Paul, in 1906, was no help. They fought it out for nine years, then Nora filed for divorce, making what the Philadelphia *North American* called "serious charges." Nora gathered up the children and sailed for her native England.

The trip was not one of joy but of terror, not rest but flight, for Andrew Mellon was right on their heels, in the person of a fleet of detectives he had employed to bring the children back: by any means necessary.

Nora McMullen was wealthy in her own right, but her money did not protect her from the predicament of being a woman alone, fleeing her husband—a situation that polite society in those days regarded as appalling.

Once in England, Nora moved from place to place, friend to friend, from the best London hotels to homes in Belgravia and Hempstead Heath, seeking refuge. She knew it was Ailsa and Paul her husband really wanted, especially Paul, the son and heir. Finally she was run to earth in Hertfordshire in 1909 where, as the *North American* reported, "hired thugs entered her home, and after beating her and a friend, took the little ones away to a home provided by the banker."

Paul and Ailsa would later remark that it had seemed their entire childhood had been dominated by the struggle between their father and mother. Nora followed her kidnapped children back to Pittsburgh but was not permitted to see them. A reporter and a cameraman took her to Andrew Mellon's home where an argument ensued. The newspapermen were beaten. Nora did not see the children.

Finally, a pre-divorce agreement was signed which called for the children to spend six months with each parent. On June 3, 1910, Andrew Mellon sullenly ushered Paul and Ailsa into his limousine for a drive to New York City where they were to be united with Nora and sail aboard the *Oceanic* for England. Andrew Mellon had agreed to the trip in the pre-divorce arrangement, but the closer the limousine came to New York City, the more he knew he could not go through with it; he feared, he later said, that their minds would be "poisoned" against him. He ordered the driver to turn around and head back to Pittsburgh.

Nora, waiting at the dock, realized what had happened. She too hurried to Pittsburgh. When she arrived at the house she simply swept through the front door, up the staircase and into the childrens' rooms before any of the servants could summon the nerve to challenge her. Although it was physically impossible for her to get the children out, she did manage to be near them for a time. The situation would get even uglier.

Andrew Mellon filed his own countersuit for divorce on September 15, 1910, and retained a battery of lawyers, among them the former Governor of Pennsylvania, William A. Stone. He also made payments to Allegheny County Prosecuting Attorney William A. Blakeley, as revealed in Harvey O'Connor's biography of Andrew Mellon, *Mellon's Millions*. Blakeley's job was to make certain that all court proceedings were kept secret. It would not do to have the name of Pittsburgh's top banker besmirched by scandal.

Paul and Ailsa favored their mother. They had never seen much of their father, not for lack of interest on his part, but because his many and varied business interests left little time for play, and because he was not by nature a warm and friendly man. Andrew Mellon loved his children, as many associates have attested, but it was difficult for the cool, reserved banker to show affection. Even the home he had built for Nora at the time of their marriage, though it overflowed with servants—cook, butler, nurse, coachman, kitchen maid, parlor maid, upstairs maid— lacked a human, personal touch.

"The house," Paul remembered later, "was late Victorian and very dark—the halls were dark, the walls were dark, and outside, Pittsburgh itself was very dark."

Andrew Mellon was accustomed to rough-and-tumble fights, and he treated the divorce as if it were a fight to the death with a business competitor.

He felt justified: the children's futures were at stake, their upbringing, the ideas which, encouraged now, would flower and bear fruit in their maturity. He especially wanted to control the way Paul would be raised. The Puritan Ethic—work—had to be ingrained early. If Paul would not take over what he and Judge Mellon had built, then he would deem a good deal of everything he aspired to a failure.

In addition, like most successful people, Andrew Mellon did not take losing lightly. And lose he might if the divorce were tried in front of a jury.

Andrew Mellon went to Boies Penrose, undisputed boss of Pennsylvania politics, a man later proven by the Senate Privileges and Elections Committee investigation of 1912 to have been on the payroll of Standard Oil at the same time he was on the public payroll. Andrew Mellon, a financial backer of Penrose, had his generosity repaid when his attorneys convinced Penrose to make a pliant state legislature pass—by a vote of 168–0—a special law empowering courts to appoint a "master" to hear evidence in private and to be sole arbiter of a divorce dispute.

Even with a law passed especially for him, with a "master" who could be counted on to be sympathetic, and with the cream of Pittsburgh's legal talent on his side, Andrew Mellon played things safe. He had $32,500 worth of acoustiphones installed to monitor his wife's conversations.

But even the mighty banker, the financial power behind such corporate behemoths as the Aluminum Company, Union Trust, and Gulf Oil, could not stop publicity. No Pittsburgh paper, even though all of them were aware of the story—and the acoustiphones—and the enormous interest it would have for readers, printed a word about the divorce proceeding. Fortunately for Nora, other Eastern newspapers did run the story, and these papers were grabbed up by a sensation-seeking public as soon as they were delivered at Pittsburgh railroad stations.

Publicity began to pay off for Nora. Actually, it was her only weapon. There was no doubt the court would rule in Andrew Mellon's favor if the proceeding was kept secret. Now, with all Pittsburgh reading her account, there seemed hope.

"My first great disillusionment," Nora told the Allegheny County Court, "came when I learned that his people were not of his people at all. I had dreamed of another Hertfordshire, with Hertfordshire lads and lassies; I had arrived in a strange land with strange people, strangers in the strange land. 'They are foreign, Huns and Slavs, and such as that, and you can't do anything with them,' I was told about the people whose affection I had dreamed of winning for my children. It was not only men. There were women and children, too, all toilers in my husband's vineyard; but none of them given the laborer's recognition; toiling and working on the estate and adding to its wealth, but not recognized as part of it. The whole community spirit was as cold and hard as the steel it made, and chilled the heart to the core. . . . Nights that I spent in my baby boy's bedroom, nursing thoughts of his future, my husband, locked in his study, nursed his dollars, millions of dollars, maddening dollars, nursed larger and bigger at the cost of priceless sleep, irretrievable health and happiness. Always new plans, bigger plans for new dollars, bigger dollars, dollars that robbed him and his family of the time we could have devoted far more profitably to a mere 'Thank God, we are living.' "

It is difficult to imagine two people less suited for marriage to each other than Andrew Mellon and Nora McMullen. She was sensitive and pretty, enjoyed good times, yearned for the rolling green hills of her native England. He cared nothing for those who worked for him, a good time was making money, and the soot-blackened skies of Pittsburgh were his idea of beauty.

All Pittsburgh was talking about the case. Pennsylvania legislators scrambled over one another trying to explain to an irate public that they had not understood that the divorce law they had passed benefited only one man. The court, bowing to overwhelming public sentiment, ruled that Nora was entitled to a jury trial.

Andrew Mellon decided to settle. His name was reviled in Pittsburgh. The people he ruthlessly exploited identified with what his young wife had been saying: "It crept over me then that perhaps I, too, a foreigner like his Huns and Slavs, had been weighed coldly, dispassionately, on the scales of demand and supply and as a wife ranked merely as a commodity in the great plans of this master financier's lifework. The babies were there: even the male heir was there. Was the wife to be laid off like other hired help when the steel mills shut down?"

The settlement gave each parent custody of Ailsa and Paul for six months out of the year. What happened in the aftermath of the settlement, however, certainly favored Andrew Mellon more than it did Nora. Anyone interested in the divorce can examine Andrew Mellon's charges against his wife, which included adultery, but her replies were withdrawn "for examination" and have never been returned to the records.

Paul Mellon was five years old when the divorce became official on July 2, 1912, and soon it was clear that he was more McMullen than Mellon. An example was the way each parent regarded art. Andrew Mellon was an accumulator of valuable paintings (his collection was

later donated to start Washington's National Gallery),
but the paintings were more an investment and a means
of maintaining status than an interest in the great
masters. For instance, a *coup* Andrew Mellon never tired
of boasting about was when he sold a $54,000 Turner to
his friend Henry Frick for $100,000.

Paul, on the other hand, would develop a genuine
appreciation of art masterpieces. He remembered how
even at an early age paintings were his friends: "There
were one or two English landscapes, and about ten of
those formal portraits. These very urbane and always
self-confident personages in their classical landscapes and
autumnal parklands smiled down at me with what
seemed a warm and friendly glow."

In reality, the characters of grandfather, father, and
son in the Mellon family would turn out to be not that
much different from other very wealthy families. Old
Judge Mellon, grasping, bigoted, narrow-minded, produced Andrew, shrewd, unprincipled, powerful, who in
turn produced Paul, cultured, lazy, hedonistic. Each
was a product of his environment.

Judge Mellon really believed the Puritan Ethic. He
was self-righteous, crude, blatantly opinionated. Andrew
Mellon did not believe it but he was not above using it
for his own ends. He was cynical, selfish, and because of
his greater power, more ruthless. Paul neither believed
in the Puritan Ethic (how could he when he himself
never worked) nor did he preach it. He appreciated his
wealth and used it for personal enjoyment, leaving the
more unsavory aspects of direct exploitation to others.

Judge Mellon would publish an autobiography pointing out exactly what he believed. Andrew Mellon would
go to great lengths to retrieve every single copy (for-

tunately, a few eluded him) because it was so clearly ultrareactionary, yet he would openly grant tax favors to himself and his rich friends. Paul Mellon would say nothing, letting public relations experts sugarcoat where the fortune came from and what it was being used for.

Judge Mellon would justify a war by saying that the Bible revealed that there would always be wars, and that, besides, America was bringing Christianity to the natives. Andrew Mellon would talk about "manifest destiny" and "saving the world for democracy." Paul Mellon would keep his mouth shut.

From very early on Paul rejected the idea of personally supervising the Mellon empire. Even if no more money was made there was enough for a hundred generations of luxury, and the fact was that more money would be made, regardless of whether he supervised or not. The United States had grown powerful, the need for a puritan ethic, at least for those who already had a fortune, seemed ludicrous.

Rare is the inheritor of great wealth who will devote the hours his ancestors did to the family fortune. An exception is David Rockefeller, chairman of Chase Manhattan Bank, heir to the Standard Oil fortune. David, when he is not traveling around the world looking for new business opportunities, is like clockwork when it comes to showing up at the bank. Said a friend of Paul Mellon: "To be blunt, Paul considers David Rockefeller to be a grind."

Paul probably would not have followed in Andrew Mellon's footsteps no matter who his mother had been, but the truth is that Nora had a large influence on what Paul would become. Paul spent summers with her in England, where there were "laughing ladies in white with gay parasols, men in impeccable white flannels and striped blazers, and always behind them, behind everything, the grass was green."

The months he spent in Pittsburgh were different. Andrew Mellon's reserve replaced Nora's warmth. Paul noted that his father never smiled, indeed, so serious was the expression on his face that it seemed it would crumble into pieces if he made the effort.

If Andrew Mellon was cold and distant, Pittsburgh was downright threatening. It was always night in the City of Iron and Steel, the sun might as well have burned out. As an adult Paul would spend a good deal of time avoiding the city where he was raised. As Lincoln Steffens pointed out, citizens called Pittsburgh "Mellon's Patch" as they choked on soot and coal dust, caught tuberculosis breathing the gas and carbon, were tormented by fiery cinders belched into the air by steel blast furnaces.

"I was happier in England," recalled Paul Mellon when he was an adult.

"It's not so much that he loved England," said a former secretary. "He hated Pittsburgh. Even now, now that it's cleaned up, he hates going back."

The Wilmington *Morning News* revealed that almost two hundred tons of soot fell monthly on each square mile of the city. Windows were blackened by coal dust and no one wore light clothing. Lincoln Steffens described Pittsburgh as "hell with the lid lifted" and "smoke by day, a pillar of fire by night."

One young newspaper reporter, Herbert Kubly, on his first night in Pittsburgh, witnessed a huge explosion in the sky, then a massive fire that seemed to hover above the entire city. He called his editor, thinking he was onto the story of his life, only to learn that what he had witnessed was commonplace, that it was caused by the blast furnaces of Jones and Laughlin Steel.

"A month in Pittsburgh," a visitor told *Time* magazine, "would justify anyone in committing suicide."

Andrew Mellon acquired a second house (the house of Paul's birth had stood on a five-acre wooded hill on Forbes Avenue, now the site of Carnegie-Mellon University) in 1917. The second house was a forty-room mansion on Woodland Road. Outside was a tennis court, a stable for horses, formal gardens. There was a huge ballroom inside, and a swimming pool and bowling alley.

All the luxury could not screen out the absence of a mother, or the grim reality of Iron City. It was lonely in the big house. Window cleaners worked full time and even when the glass was clear there was nothing to see but grey twilight.

Andrew Mellon was fighting a losing battle trying to convince his son to be like him. What was the purpose, Paul wondered. He had everything without working. Servants spoiled him, food was plentiful, even adults treated him with respect. "The adults treated him with respect," said a Pennsylvania businessman, "because they knew that some day he would be more powerful than a king."

Paul was a reluctant king. A king has people hanging on every move, every word, and Paul, even at an early age, did not want to accept responsibility for the king's subjects: that should be left to others; he wanted to reign but not to rule.

Paul looked forward to summers with his mother in England, and horses, the fine horses which already had attracted his fancy, and books, not the bank's books his father talked endlessly about, but classics.

Paul wanted the type of life Nora led, but his education was typically Pittsburgh upper class. He was chauffeured each day to Pittsburgh's exclusive Shady Side Academy, a school Andrew Mellon deliberately chose for him because it emphasized obedience to parental authority and respect for established order. It was not until Paul was twelve that he was able to begin to sort out the conflicting pulls on his life.

Five

PAUL MELLON SPENT SIX YEARS, HIS TWELFTH THROUGH his seventeenth, at the Choate Academy in Wallingford, Connecticut. At age twelve Andrew Mellon had already been learning the intricacies of banking, but Paul showed no similar bent. He enjoyed the sort of life his mother had shown him. It was hard for him to understand why his father pushed and pushed for more money and power.

On his own for the first time, Paul found a real alternative to banking and industry. "At Choate," he said, "I think I came awake a little. I got interested, really interested, in literature and in writing." Paul remained grateful to Choate his entire life. Through the years he has donated millions of dollars to the school.

Andrew Mellon was not happy with his son. He grumbled about the boy's lack of initiative, his disinterest in economics and economic theory. He thought Paul would be a laughingstock, and that people would laugh at him also. He had already lost his wife. Must he lose his son, too? Andrew Mellon believed, as Judge Mellon had, that most education was a waste of time.

But Paul would not be diverted. When he graduated from Choate he first chose to enter Princeton, then changed his mind and decided to go to Yale, chiefly because "I had been hearing about the good English Department. . . .I finally worked up enough courage to call Father in Washington—he was in the Treasury—and tell him that Yale was my real choice. I have never regretted the change."

Paul always called Andrew Mellon "Father," and it took courage on his part to make that call. He felt intimidated by Andrew Mellon, by the family fortune, by the fact that he was expected one day to run it. This he did not want to do. He wanted to enjoy, to pursue his own interests. The more Andrew Mellon chided him, the more he retreated into books.

When Paul entered Yale he was slightly above medium height, had a large patrician nose, dark complexion. He was intense, brooding, sensitive, unworldly inasmuch as he had no desire to use his education to find a place in the business world. It was, rather, a way to immerse himself in the cultured, gentlemanly, Old World sort of existence Nora McMullen loved.

Yale shielded Paul from the madness of the Roaring Twenties. He did not have to witness the squalid shacks of Pittsburgh, the bitter strikes, the insanity of the middle class as it gobbled up watered stocks and worthless securities. On the sedate campus, surrounded by other genteel sons of the wealthy, he could retreat from all that, and especially from the harangues of his father.

Paul was a brilliant student at Yale. In his first year—1925—he won the school's top prize for English literature. He wrote essays, did a learned thesis on Donn Byrne, was the first member of his class to have his poems published. He was an English honors student, a member of the Scroll and Key Senior Society, the Yale News, the Yale Literary Magazine, the University Club, the Sword and Gun Club, and Mohicans.

Paul's years at Yale reinforced his belief that Nora McMullen's philosophy of life was the correct one. It was also the easier one, the more pleasant. To Paul money seemed merely a means to acquire valuable paintings, statues. Money meant he could travel all over the world in pursuit of beautiful things. Money offered leisure, time to create his own art and to appreciate that of others. But money used to make more money, to obtain properties and sell them for a profit, to take over businesses and foreclose on homes, to expand one concern into another, to spend one's life amid the crush and roar of industry—no, it was too frightening. Let someone else do it. Andrew Mellon, seeing what his son intended to become, looked on aghast; when they were together each mirrored the dismay in the other's eyes.

When Paul returned to Pittsburgh for vacations, or went to Washington where his father was Secretary of the Treasury, he was aware not only of Andrew Mellon's contempt, but the contempt of those around the Great Man. Here he was being offered a great empire, and he was too weak and vacillating to take it.

"Paul never really stood up to his father," said Paul's former secretary. "He was afraid of him. He thought something bad might happen, that he might even lose his inheritance. Yet he couldn't bring himself to go into the business. It didn't interest him, and even if it had he knew he didn't have the mind for it."

Paul graduated from Yale in 1929 and decided he

wanted to spend a year studying history at Clare College in Cambridge. He hesitated to face the storm he knew would come when he told his father, and, as a matter of fact, it was only after promising to try his hand at the bank after a year studying in England that he received Andrew Mellon's reluctant permission.

Paul could have just defied his father, and he still would not have had to work a day in his life. Nora Mc-Mullen had plenty of money and she would have approved wholeheartedly any move that pulled her son away from her former husband. But Paul did not want such a break. He did indeed want the great Mellon inheritance; he simply did not want the responsibility of administering it.

The year at Clare College convinced Paul once and for all that he could not keep his end of the bargain. By the time he had returned to the United States in July, 1930, he had decided to enter the publishing business. He was himself a fairly talented writer, and the thought of rubbing shoulders with other intellectuals was extremely appealing. He stepped off the ship in New York City and told reporters, "Commerce and banking hold no particular interest for me. I think it is wiser for me to enter a field which is more attractive. There are other members of the family who are more fitted than I am to look after the family interests. I have certain ideas of my own about the business of book publishing and I shall try to put them into execution when I am actually connected with a publishing firm."

The *Pittsburgh Press* described the dilemma facing Paul's father: "Andrew Mellon, Secretary of the United States Treasury and one of the richest men in the world, is understood to be facing a problem more perplexing to him than the intricacies of the next income tax reduction or the consolidation of Western Pennsylvania banks under Mellon leadership.

"Mellon is confronted with the statement of his son, Paul, that the young man does not wish to enter the banking business and assume the helm of the mighty financial ship of the house of Mellon. . . .

"However, it is known that Andrew Mellon has other plans in store for him and as soon as Paul arrives here today he is to report to the Mellon Bank, where he will be given a desk and taught the fundamentals of the banking business upon which the enormous fortune of his father was built."

Paul arrived in Pittsburgh July 8 and Harvey O'Connor described the meeting between father and son: "The head of the house of Mellon summoned all the passion in his shrunken body as he exhorted, entreated, lectured the obdurate youth. Was it for this that Thomas Mellon had endured grinding poverty to win a footing in the professions, was it for this that Andrew Mellon had worked unceasingly all his life long, to see his family relapse into the obscurity from which it had come, to see his fortune scattered to the four winds?"

Paul crumbled before his father's attack. He was escorted to the bank the next morning promptly at 10:30, was introduced around by Andrew Mellon, then tried to salvage some self-respect by telling newsmen, in effect, that his father had not won entirely: "There is nothing I can say about myself right now as nothing has been decided. I'm going to be back at the bank this summer and go back to Cambridge this fall for another year. After that—well, there really isn't anything definite."

It was clear Paul was not happy that summer. He pushed papers around and did no real work and was bombarded by phone calls from his father in Washington urging him to get involved.

Paul did get away several weekends to visit his mother at the Rokeby Farm in Virginia, one of the oldest, largest, and most magnificent pieces of real estate in the nation. Andrew Mellon had purchased the Rokeby Farm for Nora McMullen at his son's urging, and it is in that grand Virginia hunt country that Paul still spends a large portion of his time.

While commuting to the bank in Pittsburgh Paul lived in the huge family mansion on Woodland Road, twenty minutes by automobile from the city's center. The mansion had forty enormous rooms, not including the fifteen bathrooms, and it was a lonely life for Paul, even though there were so many servants: "They were bumping into each other," said one observer.

Besides the tennis court, swimming pool, bowling alleys, and horse stables, Paul could enjoy the marble or carved-oak fireplaces that graced almost every room, the $40,000 automobile made of aluminum, the aluminum dressing room, the elevators that whisked people three stories up, or to the basement, the twenty-seven-acre grounds dotted with stately maples, willows, and oaks. At night the grounds were illuminated by gas lamps, and guards with guns were posted to keep away the curious.

Andrew Mellon was in Washington performing his duties at the Treasury Department most of the time that summer, but it was not *his* absence that made Paul yearn for Virginia, and Cambridge in the fall.

Paul returned to Cambridge in September, 1930, and was graduated the following year with highest honors. The degree granted was a B.A. in history. It was not until December, 1931, after much stalling, that he submitted to his father's demands and returned to the bank. It was painful that first day back on the job to have to answer the reporters' questions.

"What are you going to do?"

"I'm going to learn the banking business."

"In what capacity?"

"Whatever they want me to do."

"Under whom will you work?"

"I don't know yet."

"What about those earlier reports about your literary ambitions?"

"That's old stuff."

Paul was asked how his first day went. "I didn't do much, really," he said. "Just looked around, mostly."

Paul objected to pictures being taken, to the fuss made over him. He was also afraid of what Andrew Mellon would think: "My father—well, my father simply doesn't like that sort of thing at all."

Paul was asked to pose behind a desk. "Oh, no, no, no. Why everybody on earth would know it was a dreadful fake. They know it isn't my desk. They know I haven't any desk. I'm not a banker, and everybody knows it."

The reporters disliked Paul. He spoke "prissily." His voice was affected. He sounded more like a comedian portraying a spoiled aristocrat than the genuine aristocrat he was.

Paul's duties at the bank were vague. He was "learning the business" according to Mellon publicity men. Actually he was champing at the bit to return to Virginia, to England, to anywhere but suffocating Pittsburgh.

"He hated the work at the bank," a friend recalled. "God only knows what pressure he was under from his father."

Andrew Mellon tried to add incentive. Surely there was something of himself in his son. He decided that a touch of responsibility might awaken dormant instincts. Within a few months Paul found himself appointed to the board of directors of the National Bank of Charleroi, Pa.; Pittsburgh Coal Company; First National Bank of Donora, Pa.; and the Donora Trust Company.

The directorships would prove strictly honorary. Paul was at the bank solely to please his father; his resistance to a career in finance had been so stiffened by an easy life and Nora and schooling and a measure of success at writing that even had he tried with everything in him he probably could not have learned the business.

Paul made one half-hearted attempt to become an entrepreneur. In 1932, at age twenty-five, he and several acquaintances went into the restaurant business. It turned out to be, as *Fortune* magazine said, "as embarrassing a business fiasco as any Mellon ever experienced in Pittsburgh."

The restaurants Paul and his friends opened were in trouble from the beginning; 1932 was a depression year and people were not eating out. "In an effort to fend off bankruptcy," one of the partners later recalled, "we had our wives sitting in the windows at the noon hour, munching hamburgers and hot dogs, hoping that people would think we had begun to attract a classy line of trade."

The restaurants closed in six months. The sheriff had to sell the fixtures to meet creditor claims. If Andrew Mellon was dismayed, he kept it to himself.

But Paul was more than dismayed. He was downright ashamed. His father could manage billions, run a country's economy, and he couldn't even succeed with a pair of hamburger joints. It was clear he was the sort of person who would make $500,000 a day staying away from work, but that he would lose that much if he showed up.

Paul resented his father and the impossible demands the man made on him, but such was hardly the case with his sister Ailsa. She possessed none of the family's traditional reserve. When Andrew Mellon left Pittsburgh to go to Washington, Ailsa went along and she was in her glory. She was hostess at lavish parties thrown by her father, basked in the limelight of Washington social twirls, events that Paul went to extreme lengths to avoid. He disliked the bankers and lobbyists and bureaucrats who sang Andrew Mellon's praises over stiff drinks while bellying closer to the old man in hopes of a favor.

"If only Ailsa could have been a man!" Andrew Mellon must have thought. Ailsa was tall and thin and bony, angular, and she was always at Andrew Mellon's side, interested, even fascinated, in the corporate miracles her father had wrought. She was at home with "his people." When in June, 1926, she married David Kirkpatrick Este Bruce, son of a U.S. senator from Maryland whose family was deep into agriculture and banking, Andrew Mellon gave what *The New York Times* called "the most notable wedding Washington has ever seen."

There were two thousand guests of honor at the wedding, including President Coolidge and a number of U.S. Supreme Court Justices, senators, and representatives. Ailsa's gown had a nine-foot train and around her neck were pearls valued at $100,000. Andrew Mellon's gift to the bride was reported to be cash—$10 million!

The press of America was destined to fall in love with Paul Mellon's brother-in-law, David K. E. Bruce. The *New Republic* would call him a "diplomat's diplomat." *U.S. News and World Report* described him as a "patient, unflappable, civilized patrician." *Life* magazine saw him as a "Renaissance Man."

The truth was more prosaic. Paul's brother-in-law began his career as a diplomatic courier and one of his first assignments was to deliver a baby grand piano to the YMCA in Istanbul, Turkey. Bruce fell asleep and the piano was stolen.

David Bruce enjoyed practical jokes. Before marrying Ailsa, and perhaps living out a fantasy, he took out a Baltimore marriage license to wed a nonexistent Miss Regina Mellon. His father, Senator Bruce, called it a "mistake," his mother dismissed it as a "prank," and anyway, he did in the end marry a Mellon wealthier than any queen.

Paul Mellon enjoyed his brother-in-law's lighthearted nature although the two men were, in terms of interests and temperament, worlds apart. While Paul spent his adulthood exploring the timeless realms of great art and gave himself to the patient pursuit of great masterpieces, David K. E. Bruce was busy constructing a towering diplomatic career. He was the only man ever to hold all three of this country's most prestigious ambassadorial posts: England, France, and West Germany. He also served in both the Maryland and Virginia legislatures, was an OSS colonel during World War II, an assistant secretary of commerce, undersecretary of state, chief of mission to the Marshall Plan, special envoy to the European Coal and Steel Community, and in 1970 chief negotiator at the Paris peace talks.

Paul Mellon, as quiet about politics as he was about business, never ventured an opinion in public about his country's involvement in Indochina. David Bruce was more outspoken. As early as 1950, Bruce had ranged himself with those who wanted the United States to come to the aid of the beleaguered French in Indochina. He branded those who disagreed with him "obtuse," and told the Senate Foreign Relations Committee on July 20, 1951, that "to assume the burden of colonialism is not to assume its guilt." Those who had hoped to see the United States extricate itself from the deepening quagmire of Indochina were not cheered by Bruce's appointment as chief negotiator in 1970.

Shortly after his appointment, Bruce got his mission started on the wrong foot by saying exactly the opposite of what he meant to say. A North Vietnamese proposal, he announced, "was new wine in old bottles."

David Bruce is currently America's highest-ranking diplomat in China.

David Bruce's marriage to Ailsa Mellon ended in divorce after twenty years. He later married Evangeline Bell, a woman who enjoyed the social circuit as much as Ailsa had. Theodore White described the style of David Bruce while he was Ambassador to France: "Bruce and his startlingly handsome second wife dressed as Queen and Knave of Spades at a Paris charity masquerade; Bruce dressed in green knickers out hunting with the President of France (he set the diplomatic record with a bag of ninety-nine pheasants in a single day); Bruce kissing village mayors on the cheek, praising them for their local beauties or local wines; Bruce presiding over ballet openings or art showings—was the storybook ambassador in the flesh."

Kissing village mayors and killing ninety-nine pheasants was not Paul's style. In fact, people wondered what his style was. He seldom spoke to the press, rarely entertained, was hardly ever seen in public. When Andrew Mellon went to England as ambassador to the Court of St. James, Ailsa took over with glee the job of chief hostess. Paul continued to live alone in the Woodland Road home and commute to work each day.

Paul was like Thomas and Andrew Mellon in one respect: he shared a distrust of the masses. He was not the sort to barge into a crowd of well-wishers to shake hands. If he had to live in Pittsburgh to please his father, he was at least grateful for the privacy that guards and a large estate provided.

It is doubtful if the people of Pittsburgh would have enjoyed his company any more than he would have reveled in theirs. His speech was marked by long, gliding syllables; to be sure, he was cultured, but he wore it on his sleeve.

Paul threw a major party in January, 1933, and it gave curious Pittsburghers a glimpse at the tastes of Andrew Mellon's only son. The party was low-keyed, very proper. There was dinner for twenty-five, then two hundred lesser Pittsburgh socialites arrived at 11 P.M. for dancing and swimming. "Simplicity," said the *Pittsburgh Press,* "marked the affair."

Paul stuck it out at the bank for three years, a period he later considered the low mark of his life. It was a period of vicious gossip in Pittsburgh. Andrew Mellon's health was failing fast and the rumors were that Paul would stay at the bank not one day longer than his father lived. To his credit, Paul left before that, but when he did Andrew Mellon was too old and too sick to complain.

On February 2, 1935, giving the press and Pittsburgh society less than a day's notice, Paul married Mary Conover Brown, a divorcee, the daughter of a prominent Kansas City family. Mary Conover Brown attended Columbia University and the Sorbonne in Paris before graduating from Vassar.

Paul was more than two years younger than his bride.

79

She was a talented decorator and magazine writer, a sensitive, intelligent mature woman who shared Paul's interest in art and literature. Like Paul, she disliked publicity, prying reporters, ogling crowds. The marriage was a quiet affair at the David Bruce home on super-wealthy Sutton Place in New York City and was followed by a European honeymoon.

When Paul and Mary returned to Pittsburgh the city's newspapers wondered out loud if there would be a change in Iron City's social climate. Paul was, after all, young and handsome and very, very rich, and Mary was no stranger to upper-class entertaining. "Society Looks Ahead But Only Speculates," read one headline, followed by "What is in store for social Pittsburgh now that Paul Mellon is married and will live here at the home of his father Andrew W. Mellon?"

The first thing Paul and Mary did was build an eight-foot-high stockade fence around their home to keep neighbors from spying on them while they played tennis in shorts. The purpose of the fence was to avoid publicity, but its effect was just the opposite.

"What's the fence made of?" a neighbor was asked.

"Gall and wormwood," came the answer.

The fence became a *cause celebre* in Pittsburgh, much to Paul's distress. He only wanted to be left alone, to be permitted to enjoy his wealth without unpleasantness. But it was not to be. "It looks as if a prison was in our midst," complained one neighbor. "It takes us back to the old Block House days at Fort Pitt," said another, "because this isn't any mere fence. It's a real stockade."

Paul pointed out that the wood for the fence was quite tasteful, that it had been imported from France, but the tempest in a teapot continued. The armed guards who patrolled the property, neighbors complained, added to the stockade atmosphere. But the fence stayed up. It was not solely because the Mellons played tennis in shorts, as a groundskeeper explained: "Only a week ago, we had to request two young persons to leave the tennis courts. They had come with balls and racquets, believing it was a public course." Also, there were students from a nearby college who took strolls on the property: "They don't touch the flowers or cause any trouble, but it was thought best to make the grounds strictly private."

"Paul wanted to be left alone," said his former secretary. "He didn't want to be forced into a business career, and he didn't want to be forced into associations with people he did not care for."

Paul and Mary began spending less and less time in Pittsburgh, a city still as dark and unappetizing as a tomb. More often than not they were at the Upperville estate, riding horses and tending an art collection that had already become impressive. Tasteful paintings dotted every wall in the Virginia home. The horses Paul owned also had "class". Drinmore Lad was good enough to run in the Grand National at Aintree, England, and Rokeby Farm steeplechasers captured four consecutive Carolina Cups.

Paul was living the cordial, cultured, gentleman-farmer type of life he wanted. Armed guards kept people away from the estate, and there were no near neighbors to complain about "stockade atmospheres."

Paul would be the principal owner of such corporate giants as Gulf Oil, Alcoa, and the Mellon Bank, and he would grow enormously more wealthy because of them. Of course, he concerned himself little with their actual operation. There were, as he pointed out, others more fitted to run the empire. He was content to let them do it, to hide from the world, surrounded by great treasures.

He believed that he, not David Bruce, was a Renaissance Man.

Paul was not even on hand May 6, 1937, when the Mellon Institute was dedicated to

"Andrew Wm. Mellon
1855–1937

AND

Richard Beatty Mellon
1858–1933

THEY FOUNDED THE
INSTITUTE AND GAVE THIS
BUILDING FOR THE PURSUIT
OF SCIENTIFIC RESEARCH
TO BENEFIT MANKIND"

One day in 1972 someone crossed out the word MAN-KIND and substituted THEMSELVES. On the same wall an ungrateful student had written "GULF KILLS!"

Six

THE PORTUGUESE WEST AFRICAN COLONY OF ANGOLA
has 5.8 million inhabitants, more than ninety percent of
whom are black. It is a colony fourteen times the size of
Portugal, and rich in such products as oil, coffee, fish-
meal, corn, sisal, sugar, cotton, coconuts, ivory, cattle,
iron ore, diamonds, copper, manganese, sulphur, phos-
phates, gold, and tobacco.

The tiny percentage of the population that is Portuguese rules Angola with an iron hand. The *London Observer,* for example, reported that in one month, May,
1961, more Africans were killed in Angola than had
been murdered in the Union of South Africa in the last
hundred years.

Henrique Galvao, then Inspector of the Portuguese
Ministry, described the plight of Angolans in an official
1947 report: "In some ways the situation is worse than
simple slavery. Under slavery, after all, the Native is
bought as an animal: his owner prefers him to remain as
fit as a horse or an ox. Yet here the Native is not bought
—he is hired from the State, although he is called a free

man. And his employer cares little if he sickens or dies, once he is working, because when he sickens or dies, his employer will simply ask for another."

Despite a new government in Portugal, the situation has not changed much in 1974. A huge black insurrection that has been carried on since 1961, virtually unreported in the American press, has liberated much of the country. Areas of the nation that have been freed from the Portuguese have educational and medical facilities. Even areas that have not been freed are slightly better off than before. The Portuguese have been forced to institute a few minor reforms to prevent the Africans still under their domination from joining completely with the rebels. Still, the situation in Portuguese-controlled areas of Angola is colonialism at its worst.

All Africans are subject to contract (slave) labor unless "gainfully" employed, and "gainfully" does not include subsistence farming, which is universally practiced by the Angolans.

Less than one percent of the black population has the right to vote. More than ninety percent of the population, blacks are only fourteen percent of the school population. *Per capita* income for blacks is sixty dollars a year. In one recent seven-year period, more than 100,-000 blacks died at slave labor. Today fifteen-year sentences are not unusual if a black is even suspected of being sympathetic toward the guerrilla movement. Guerrillas who are captured are executed on the spot. All blacks need travel permits within their own country no matter the distance of their journey.

The recently deposed Portuguese Prime Minister, Marcelo Caetano, justified his country's colonial rule by saying: "Deep within each Portuguese there exists a firm determination to contribute toward maintaining forever (!) the Portuguese colonial community as a strong and living reality."

Former overseas Minister Dr. Adriano Moreira put it another way: "Our politics of today are the politics of yesterday."

The Caetano government was overthrown in the Spring of 1974 and replaced by a military regime headed by General Antonio de Spinola. The coup brought hundreds of thousands of Portuguese into the streets and many of Caetano's hated secret police were summarily executed by the crowds.

Spinola, who was trained by and fought with the Nazis in World War II on the Eastern Front, began negotiations with the Africans. What he proposed, however, (a "federation" with Portugal) was rejected by the liberation fighters. The wars in the colonies went on, and Portugal, the poorest country in Europe, continued to be bled by the fighting.

As *The New York Times* pointed out, one of the reasons Portugal has not been evicted entirely from Angola is that it has some 60,000 troops there. Another reason is that between 1959 and 1965 Portugal received $300 million in aid from the U.S. Government, not including the $5 million a year rent it receives for use of the big naval air base in the Portuguese Azores. In addition, U.S. officers have trained Portuguese troops in counterinsurgency methods.

But America has done more than train the Portuguese. The publication *Portugal and NATO* revealed that that country, which has no airplane manufacturing facilities whatsoever, had the following U.S.-built planes in 1970: fifty Republic F–84 G Thunderjets; fifty North American F–86F Sabres; thirty Cessna T–37s; eighteen Lockheed PV–2 Harpoons; twelve Lockheed P–2V Neptunes; and twenty Douglas B–26s.

American-built planes have for years dropped napalm, fragmentation bombs, and white phosphorous on rebellious Africans. These planes also were used to drop the chemical picloram, manufactured by Dow, to kill food supplies being grown by the guerrillas. Cacodylique acid, which contains arsenic and is lethal to humans, was also dropped on their crops.

But it was the Manchester *Guardian,* June 18, 1961, quoting missionaries, that best described what Portuguese colonialism is like: ". . . utmost barbarism, lynching and slaughtering tens of thousands of men, women and children."

The New York Times, July 7, 1968, told why Portugal clings to Angola: "Favored by nature and harassed not intolerably by a seven-year insurrection, this huge Portuguese territory on the west coast of Africa is enjoying a boom. Angola, once known for mahogany forests and gorillas and not much else, presents a transformed picture.

"Of the growing new hues in the economic picture of this overseas province of Portugal, the brightest is Cabinda, a wedge of dense, tropical forest separated from the northern tip of the territory by the Congo River.

"Oil has been discovered there in enormous quantities, the extent still not fully known. In three or four months, however, oil will be coursing through a pipeline three feet in diameter to tankers waiting ten miles out in the shallow sea.

"Even now there is enough oil to promise new wealth to the long-suffering *Portuguese* [my italics—W.H.].

There is more than enough to give a new security to the white-dominated government. . . ."

The company that has that oil concession, the company that profits from the super-exploitation of Africans, indeed the company that has dominated Angola's economy for more than a decade, is the Mellon family's—and especially Paul Mellon's—Gulf Oil. Gulf has not once been heard to raise its voice against the policies of the Portuguese. In fact, if it were not for those policies profits would not be so great. It is estimated that in 1974 alone Gulf will pay more than $40 million in royalties to the Portuguese. To the Angolans, in whose ground the oil lies, will go nothing.

William R. Cotter, President of the African-American Institute, put the issue into perspective: "There can be no doubt that the oil and mineral wealth discovered in Angola. . . during the past ten to fifteen years has immensely increased the value of these territories to the Portuguese. This increase in value undoubtedly accounts in part for the tenacity with which the Portuguese are trying to hang on to their African colonies. At the same time, it is also likely that U.S. business investment, and particularly the enormous investment of Gulf Oil in Angola, has directly contributed to the ability of the Portuguese to pay for the war, has strengthened the balance of payments for Portugal and has made the colonies ever so much more valuable than they would be without that investment."

In 1971 twenty-seven members of the U.S. Congress sent a letter to Gulf calling on the company to withdraw from Angola. At the same time a number of American church groups called for a boycott of Gulf products. Even Gulf stockholders became concerned:

in 1971 a group of them disrupted the company's annual meeting.

The U.S. Government is not likely to act against the interests of Portugal and Gulf. Portugal has proved to be too valuable a friend. In October, 1973, when President Nixon declared a worldwide military alert because of the Middle East, the only European country that would allow American supplies headed for Israel to land, was Portugal. A grateful Richard Nixon promised to increase aid to Portugal; the Arabs countered with the oil embargo.

Moral, economic, and political censures have failed to get Gulf to alter its policies in Angola; moreover, in 1974 the company announced that it was going to expand its operations in that unfortunate country.

The Portuguese East African colony of Mozambique has a population of 7.6 million people, 97.5 percent of whom are black. This potentially wealthy country produces oil, cement, flour, sugar, coconuts, cotton, copra, sisal, cashews, tantalum, coal, copper, gold, and asbestos. Mozambique is eight times the size of Portugal. If anything, the Africans there are worse off than they are in Angola.

The Portuguese have between forty thousand and sixty thousand troops in Mozambique trying to quell a liberation movement. The reason is obvious: the 2.5 percent of the population that is white consumes 33 percent of the nation's wealth. White workers, doing precisely the same work, are paid four times the wages of their black counterparts. Blacks have to carry special identification cards at all times; being caught without one means a lengthy jail sentence. Blacks caught in a "white" area after dark are shot.

Thousands of African nationalists are held by the DGS (Portuguese secret police) in concentration camps on the Island of Galinhas. Thousands more are held on the Cape Verde Islands in a camp run by Arnoldo Schultz, who received his training under the Nazis. Torture and murder are commonplace in the camps.

In 1958, out of a population of six million blacks, exactly one had a college degree.

The Portuguese call their treatment of Africans paternalistic, but a better word would be barbaric. In a letter to *Look* magazine, March 28, 1961, the attitude of the Portuguese was captured perfectly: "A certain amount of brutality exists. We admit it. But in order to be brutal to someone, you must care about him. An African is like a woman. The more you beat her, the more she loves you."

One soldier, Valentin Bom, a graduate of the Portuguese Military Academy, told about recruiting officers who described "fun in the colonies, like using Africans for target practice."

Nothing better illustrates Portuguese rule in Mozambique, however, than the June 26, 1960, demonstration by the peasants of Mueda. It was a peaceful demonstration, the peasants wanted merely a few basic rights, but the response was swift and deadly. Portuguese troops opened fire on men, women, and children, killing more than five hundred people, eight times more than were murdered in the infamous massacre at Sharpeville in South Africa.

Columbia University Professor Marvin Harris spent 1956 and 1957 in Mozambique, then described what he saw: "The Negro is regarded as an eternal child, amusing in his backwardness, sometimes loyal and hardworking, but never the complete equal of a white, never desirable as a wife though acceptable as an illicit lover; in short, a good servant when well-disciplined, who is likeable as long as he doesn't try to take your hand when you offer him a foot. These attitudes, coupled with the arbitrary beatings, the discriminatory wages, the forced labor, the curfews, the denial of freedom of movement, the unilateral contracts, the compulsory crop system, the separate and unequal educational system, and the subjection to arbitrary, personal justice on every hand, leave little room for the Portuguese or their well-wishers to maneuver."

Conditions have not changed. In January, 1974, the *London Times* announced that an estimated three hundred villagers had been executed in a single operation.

The most important force in the economy of Mozambique is Gulf Oil. It is likely that if Gulf withdrew, the Portuguese would soon be forced to withdraw. Despite strong citizen protest in this country, and the intense disapproval of African, Asian, and Latin American countries, Gulf has announced that it intends to stay in Mozambique.

The Middle East is where it's all about. Practically every political scientist in the world agrees that if World War III arrives, it will be over that volatile section of the planet. One key country is Iran.

Iran is the fourth largest oil producing nation in the world. It is a beautiful country of high mountains and salt deserts and stunning oases. The ruins of Persepolis are there, but so are modern jetports and huge dams and hydroelectric power stations. The Shah of Iran's army, supplied almost exclusively by the United States, is the most powerful in the Middle East.

In October, 1971, the Shah threw a party near the

ruins of Persepolis to celebrate twenty-five centuries of Iranian monarchy. The guests came from far and wide, from seventy countries to honor the Shah—"King of Kings" and "Light of the Aryans." The guests were housed in opulent air-conditioned tents, attended by armies of servants, gorged themselves on exotic delicacies, and were chauffeured about in Rolls Royces. Although Iran is not an Arab nation, it must have seemed to those in attendance—including America's official representative, Spiro Agnew—that the country was something straight out of *Arabian Nights*. They could not have been more wrong.

Iran's principal city, Teheran, did not even have a sewer system. Most of the people in that fabulous oil-rich land are impoverished and illiterate. Many are starving. Many universities are constantly being closed by the SAVAK (Iranian secret police) to prevent anti-government activity. It is true that in the past year and a half the Shah has plunged some of his oil revenue into building up the feudal economy (he is trying to create a middle class as a buffer against the poor) but Iran's poor remain virtually unaffected.

Prior to the Shah's party more than twenty-five hundred students believed to be opposed to his regime were rounded up and jailed without charge. A spokesman for the Iranian embassy said there are more than ten thousand Iranian students in the United States. A number of these have participated in anti-Shah demonstrations in America and have been tried *in absentia* in Iran and sentenced to up to ten years in prison.

There were guests at the party the Shah threw who wore diamonds the size of golf balls on their foreheads.

Many Jewish people are concerned that the U.S. may

be willing to barter away the security of Israel. They point out that Israel may be expendable, since America has an even more powerful ally in the Middle East—Iran—and one that does not heat the blood of the Arabs as much as Israel does.

The truth is that the Shah has reason to trust the United States: he would not even be in power were it not for American help.

On March 15, 1951, the Iranian people voted to nationalize the country's oil and a month later Mohammed Mossadegh became Prime Minister. Mossadegh immediately began carrying out the electorate's will by expropriating British holdings (at the time England held a near-monopoly on Iranian oil). Authors David Wise and Thomas B. Ross in their book *The Invisible Government* described what happened: "There is no doubt at all that the CIA organized and directed the 1953 coup that overthrew Premier Mohammed Mossadegh and kept Shah Mohammed Reza Pahlevi on the throne. But few Americans know that the coup that toppled the government of Iran was led by a CIA agent who was the grandson of President Theodore Roosevelt."

The man's name was Kermit "Kim" Roosevelt, and authors Wise and Ross revealed what his actions accomplished: "In the aftermath, the British lost their monopoly on Iran's oil. In August, 1958, an international consortium of Western Oil companies signed a twenty-five-year pact [with an additional fifteen-year option] with Iran for its oil. Under it, the former Anglo-Iranian Oil Company got 40 percent, a group of American oil companies [including Gulf] got 40 percent, Royal Dutch Shell got 14 percent and the Compagnie Francaise des Petroles 6 percent."

Allen Dulles, former head of the CIA, as much as admitted that the U.S. toppled Mossadegh. He wrote in his book *The Craft of Intelligence* that "support from the outside was given. . . to the Shah's supporters" without actually naming the CIA.

At his party the Shah gave the impression that he was the direct descendant of twenty-five centuries of family monarchy. In reality, the first relative of his to hold the throne was his father, Reza Khan, who came to power in a 1925 coup. The Shah's father is best remembered for having spent every cent of money received for Iranian oil between 1927 and 1940 on arms.

The first thing the present Shah did after being put back in power by the CIA was to hire General Fazlollah Zahedi as Prime Minister. Zahedi, the recipient of almost every medal the Hitler government could confer, promptly turned Iran into a police state.

With Mossadegh out of the way, Iranian politics went back on a business-as-usual basis. Little of the vast oil income ever reached the people, and most of the $1.3 billion in aid the U.S. sent the Shah stuck in the pockets of decadent government officials.

Today the Shah holds forth on CBS's "Sixty Minutes," philosophizing on the glory of monarchy and the evils of democracy. He also gave an interview to Oriana Fallaci in October, 1973, in which he said that the Prophet Ali had appeared to him in a vision. He also told the Italian journalist: "I believe in God, and that I have been chosen by God to perform a task. My visions were miracles that saved the country. My reign has saved the country, and it has done so because God was on my side."

Actually, it was the U.S. who was on his side. But the Shah was not the only one who benefitted: so did Kermit Roosevelt. Around the CIA he is still respectfully referred to as "Mr. Iran."

He was rewarded by Gulf Oil, too. In 1960 he was made a vice-president of the company.

Not all sheiks and sultans have always been wealthy. The *Overseas News Agency,* June 17, 1953, revealed that many had incomes of about ten dollars a month, "earned" by stopping travelers passing through their land and assessing a toll. The Sheik of Kuwait was doing little better than that before oil was discovered in his country in 1938.

Kuwait is only one-seventh the size of the State of Pennsylvania and produces about 15 percent of the world's oil. There are only 830,000 residents of Kuwait, *per capita* income is enormous (yet most of the people are poor), and in size it is by far the greatest oil producer on earth.

In 1899 the Sheik signed a treaty with Great Britain promising never to sell mineral rights in Kuwait without English approval. In 1913 he renewed the pledge. Then came 1932 and hints of oil. Andrew Mellon took the hint and there were rumors that he was negotiating with the Sheik behind England's back. Naturally, the British protested. A diplomatic furor ensued, with the U.S. Government siding with Gulf. It was not surprising since Andrew Mellon was still in America's employ, as Herbert's Hoover's ambassador to the Court of St. James.

Nobody expected Kuwait to turn out as rich as it did. Nevertheless, negotiations were continued, too slowly for Andrew Mellon. "The delay," he said, while still an ambassador, "in reaching a settlement in the matter of the Kuwait oil concessions" was "becoming exasperating."

The English pointed out that any sort of negotiations were illegal, since they had Kuwaiti mineral rights tied up *in perpetuity*. Andrew Mellon kept negotiating.

A deal was made. Great Britain was in no position to

try to out-muscle the United States, and the United States was clearly backing Andrew Mellon. The Kuwait Oil Company was founded in 1933, owned equally by Gulf and Anglo, and the obliging Sheik granted a seventy-five-year concession covering the whole of the country. The deal the Sheik made may perhaps be recorded as history's worst.

Oil was discovered in the Burgan Field in 1938, and the discovery was enormous! It was the greatest single oil find in history, and it dwarfed Spindletop. World War II and fear of German bombing were the reasons production did not get underway at the Burgan Field in earnest until 1946, when six million barrels were produced. This shot up to 126 million barrels in 1950, 348 million in 1954, then to 500 million and more.

In one year alone Gulf's profits from Kuwait, according to *Business Week,* April 14, 1956, were $160 million.

Things got better. *Time,* September 20, 1963, reported that Gulf—"whose cashbox is bulging from oil gushers in Kuwait"—was expanding into other businesses. Some of those businesses were rubber, fertilizer, housing, chemicals, asphalt, coal, and auto supplies.

In the late 1940s and early 1950s Gulf became primarily an international company. Gulf's 1955 annual report revealed that in 1946 the company produced 87 million barrels of crude oil domestically, 35 million barrels elsewhere. In 1955 there was a complete turnabout. The company's domestic production remained about the same, while 252 million barrels were produced elsewhere. In 1969 Gulf produced 523,670,000 barrels in the U.S., and in Kuwait (one-fourth the size of Pennsylvania) 1.4 billion barrels!

Clearly, Gulf was not responding to Congressional efforts to emphasize domestic production.

If *per capita* income in Kuwait is misleading, it is

nonetheless true that the Emir Sabah al-Salim al-Sabah, the country's ruler, is rolling in money, as are his relatives.

The people as a whole, however, are poor, and even worse off are those who toil in Gulf's oil fields. The Kuwait oil workers are imported from India, Pakistan, and Saudi Arabia; mainly they are imported so that the heaviest exploitation does not fall on native Kuwaitis, who might rebel, but on "foreigners."

Emir Sabah al-Salim al-Sabah has a certain *chutzpah.* His Ministry of Guidance and Information has published a book titled, *Kuwait Today; A Welfare State.*

The loss of the Persian Gulf and the profits such companies as Gulf extract from it would be almost incalculable. Writing in the *New Statesman,* Paul Johnson said the loss of such profits "could inflict a mortal blow at our world trading position." Said C. L. Sulzberger in *The New York Times:* "It is a paradox of this anticolonial era that if Britain's Empire were suddenly to relinquish its appanages in the Persian Gulf, NATO and the free world might collapse."

Venezuela has only ten million people and is one of the world's largest oil-producing, oil-exporting nations; yet the majority of people there live in dire poverty. Since 1955, according to John Gerassi, former Latin American correspondent for *Time* magazine, diphtheria and encephalitis and typhoid have been on the rise.

Gerassi, in his best-selling book *The Great Fear in Latin America,* describes an all too typical scene in Venezuela: "We were able to start a conversation with a small mild-mannered man of forty-odd years who told us that three families—sixteen children—lived in his one-room shack made of discarded or stolen planks. It was a hot and humid day, and almost automatically we began to stare with him at a fifty-foot-wide Coca-Cola advertisement that stood out at the foot of the slum hill. 'None of us in this house has ever drunk a Coca-Cola,' he said softly. 'One day we will kill those who make them.' "

But it is not Coca-Cola that is chiefly responsible for the poverty of Venezuelans. It is the oil companies, the Standard group, Shell, and Gulf. Through Mene Grande Oil Company, another Delaware corporation taking advantage of that DuPont-controlled state's tax shelters, Gulf extracts as much as 200,000 barrels of oil a day from Venezuelan soil. Incredibly, Gulf pays its stockholders more money in dividends than it pays out in wages and salaries in Venezuela.

Gulf is hardly an American goodwill ambassador. Hatred of Gulf's exploitation of their resources was one of the reasons an angry crowd of Venezuelans surrounded Vice-President Richard Nixon's car in 1958 in Caracas, smashed its windows, and threw stones at him. Nixon's face was cut, he was white and shaken; only quick action on the part of his driver saved his life. Hatred was also one of the reasons, in 1969, why the Venezuelan government had to cancel a planned visit by Nelson Rockefeller. Students had seized university buildings and there was street fighting with rocks and pistols.

Former President Romulo Betancourt, visiting the United States after a coup had overthrown him, walked past the National Gallery of Art in Washington, D.C., donated by Andrew Mellon. Betancourt said that the inscription on the building ought to read: "Gift of the Venezuelan people to the capital of the United States."

There is one doctor for every twenty-one hundred people in Venezuela. Less than one percent of the population completes high school. The country has one of the worst balance of payments and balance of trade in the world. The rich people who live in Venezuela trade their oil for cigarettes, whisky, and yachts. Products that would be useful to a broad spectrum of the populace—food, clothing, building materials—are in scandalous short supply.

Life expectancy for a Venezuelan is forty-nine years. The *per capita* consumption of oil is nine times higher in the U.S. than in Venezuela.

Most sinister of all is the fact that Venezuela oil reserves are likely to be exhausted in ten years. The big oil companies—Gulf, Standard, Shell—need only go elsewhere. The people of Venezuela, who have profited little from their nation's abundant natural resources, will have nowhere to go.

Angola. Mozambique. Iran. Kuwait. Venezuela. Gulf must shoulder a large portion of the blame for the wretched conditions most people in those countries are forced to endure, and for the repressive character of those nations' governments. Gulf, if it does not encourage the repression, certainly benefits from it; just as certainly, the company does not speak out against it. The repression keeps wages appallingly low, and efforts for higher pay are inevitably answered with jail, torture, even death. If the efforts are successful, as in the case of Iran, Gulf has reason to believe that the U.S. Government will intervene.

Although it is possible that Gulf does not approve of the brutal Portuguese regimes in Angola and Mozambique, or that of the luxury-loving Shah in Iran, or the decadent Sheik in Kuwait, or the military in Venezuela, the company has not been heard to raise its voice against them. Profits are taken; no questions are asked. The men who run the company are busy satisfying stockholders. The man who controls the company collects paintings, and uses armed guards to keep the people away.

In Gulf's defense, it should be pointed out that raising wages or advocating reform might lead to the company's ruin. Quite simply, if Gulf paid foreign workers higher wages, it would not be able to maintain a high profit margin. Competitors like Standard Oil and Shell—with less expensive production costs—would undersell Gulf and drive it out of business. Not only would the prices of Standard and Shell be lower if Gulf paid higher wages, but stockholders would desert Gulf in droves to reinvest their money in companies with a more "profit-oriented" outlook.

Gulf is in dozens of countries around the world, makes money in those countries, large sums of money, yet people who live in those countries barely subsist. Gulf's financial investment in these nations is not as large as in Kuwait or Angola, and therefore the influence the company has over the governments is proportionately less, but the point is that Gulf has no qualms whatsoever about doing business with some of the worst tyrants on earth. Nor does the country raise its voice a decibel to protest what happens in those countries. As mentioned, to do so would be to risk profits.

Gulf is in Colombia, a country with a *per capita* income of $300 a year, despite being rich in oil and coffee. There is one doctor for every 2,900 people in Colombia (in the U.S. there is one for every 780), many of the people work on land owned by others and are paid *nothing,* twelve percent of the population owns ninety-two percent of the land, fifty percent have never seen the inside of a classroom—because, as one businessman put it, "education leads to ideas"—and since 1948, in a country of 20 million, more than 300,000 people have been killed in a civil war between rival government factions. Life expectancy in Colombia is forty-four years (in the United States it is about seventy).

Gulf is in Bolivia, a country with a *per capita* income of $150 a year. Fifty-eight percent of Bolivia's population is illiterate and there is one doctor for every 3,900 people. In September, 1969, in an effort to keep some of its resources at home, a popular front government seized power and began to nationalize Gulf holdings. Happily for Gulf, a coup engineered by troops trained in the United States overthrew the government in 1971 and restored the old order. *Business Week* remarked that the main beneficiary of the 1971 coup would appear to be Gulf, whose holdings were expected to be fully restored.

Gulf is in the Congo-Kinshasa (Zaire) and enjoys the cooperation of a military dictatorship headed by General Joseph D. Mobutu. There is no political freedom whatsoever in the Congo-Kinshasa. Elections under General Mobutu are unheard of. The Congo-Kinshasa is one of the most backward, disease-plagued nations in the world. Illiteracy and destitution and starvation are the rule of the day in this potentially wealthy nation of 17 million.

Gulf is in Paraguay, a country headed by the notorious Alfredo Stroessner, where *per capita* income is less than $100 a year. There are more soldiers and police in Paraguay than workers. Leprosy is a common disease. Life expectancy is thirty-two years. Political prisoners are tortured and murdered in the Chaco Island concentration camp. Defending U.S. support of Stroessner, whose top aides have been shown by a Jack Anderson investigation to be drug smugglers, an American embassy official said: "In the last analysis, our policy is one of survival. Thus a sure anti-Communist, no matter how despicable, is better than a reformer, no matter how honest, who might turn against us." Stroessner has done one thing for the predominantly Catholic population of Paraguay: he has made the Virgin Mary an honorary field marshal in the Paraguayan army.

Gulf is in South Africa, where free convict labor is used, where the apartheid regime guarantees no rights whatsoever to the predominantly black population, where blacks can be arrested for no offense at all, where they are regularly referred to as "coons," "jigaboos," and "niggers," and where in 1966 alone 65,000 black children starved to death. Even elevators are segregated in South Africa. Tennis star Arthur Ashe was denied admission to the country. Actor Sidney Poitier had to sign a paper saying he was his producer's slave in order to make a film there. Lena Horne was kicked out. Most important, a black who tries to leave can be sentenced to death.

Gulf is in Brazil, another military dictatorship, this one headed by General Emilio G. Medici. Torture, including the picana, an electrical device which when attached to nipples or testes causes insanity, is employed by the police. Starvation in the populous northeast of Brazil rivals that of India. Police "death squads" roam the cities executing alleged enemies of the state, and then leave a Skull and Crossbones insignia on the mutilated bodies. Amnesty International, a humanitarian group interested in the freedom of political prisoners, calls Brazil's government one of the most oppressive regimes in the world. There is one doctor for every 2,500 people, and life expectancy, in a nation richer in natural resources than the United States, is thirty-six years.

Gulf is in Chile, where a recent military coup toppled the democratically elected government of Marxist President Salvador Allende. Thousands of people were murdered in the coup, and Santiago's National Stadium was the scene of daily mass executions. The leading Chilean daily newspaper, *El Mercurio,* supporting the junta that seized power, said that a "Communist Jew" should "hang from every lamp post."

Gulf is in South Vietnam, where vast reserves of off-shore oil have been discovered. Because of the discovery, a number of people contend that the company has more than a passing interest in maintaining the pro-U.S. Thieu government in power. In any case, so large is the new discovery of oil expected to be that the United States Senate is conducting an investigation into the possible role oil companies played in prolonging the conflict in Indochina. What is especially frightening is that Gulf and other companies have signed contracts with the Thieu regime—over the protests of the North Vietnamese and the Viet Cong—for offshore drilling rights. What if Thieu should fall, a not unlikely possibility? Would the U.S. move back in militarily to protect the oil companies? But that eventuality is the tip of the iceberg, as James Ridgeway pointed out in his 1973 book, *The Last Play.* Ridgeway revealed that Gulf—and other companies—have signed offshore drilling contracts with the Taiwanese government. The problem is, Taiwan signed away rights to offshore drilling on the continental shelf of Mainland China: the Mao government says the continental shelf belongs to the People's Republic.

Would the American government be willing to risk war with a nation of 800 million people because of agreements a few oil companies—controlled by a few people—signed with Chiang Kai-shek?

Seven

WHEN ANDREW MELLON DIED, THE LITTLE WORK PAUL spent on the family businesses stopped entirely. He continued to ride horses on the Upperville estate, hunted foxes, played polo, collected paintings, dabbled with poetry and essay-writing, enjoyed fine wine and rare books. He was a gentleman farmer who frequently journeyed to England to talk with royalty. They were, he knew, his type of people. They never, never, talked about money. It was bad taste.

Paul also went fishing with Ernest Hemingway in the Bahamas, wrestled with the mighty blue marlin and discussed the publishing business with the great writer. Paul was hardly the robust Hemingway type of person, but he had money and Hemingway was willing to listen.

Hemingway and Paul Mellon were an unusual pair. Hemingway had a deep distrust of the rich. He wrote that they used their money to meet celebrities so they could later name-drop in front of friends and leave the impression that somehow accomplished and gifted people found them worthwhile. On Paul's part, the hard-drinking, fast-living, outspoken Hemingway had to seem a polar opposite to the proper circles he was used to moving in.

Paul was thirty and already a connoisseur of paintings when he was appointed president of the National Gallery of Art in 1937, and he was on hand March 18, 1941, when the gallery was officially opened. President Franklin Roosevelt was there to accept the gift on behalf of the nation and among the notables present were Mrs. Woodrow Wilson, H. J. Heinz II, Senator Robert Taft, and Charles Evans Hughes. Chief Justice Hughes called the donation "a memorial to an eminent benefactor, whose patriotic ardor and love of art prompted the conception of this plan for public enrichment. It will always be a memorial to his public spirit, and it is a fitting crown to his public services."

The art collection Andrew Mellon donated was valued at $50 million. Paul said that "Now these beautiful paintings belong to everyone, and everyone will have the privilege of enjoying them."

Paul was fully aware that Andrew Mellon's gift was not as generous as it first appeared to be on the surface. Andrew Mellon announced the donation in 1936, one year after the provisions of the 1935 Revenue Act made the art collection liable for estate taxes of $32,362,000. Those taxes would have been payable in cash.

Andrew Mellon's donation served another purpose. Not only did he avoid a huge estate tax assessment, but he obtained a charitable tax deduction of tens of millions of dollars. The $50 million valuation of the paintings was Andrew Mellon's, not the amount of money he had paid for them. He contended that many of the paintings had appreciated greatly in value since he had purchased them, and that the higher valuation was the

104

correct one to be used in calculating their worth. Even at the time of the donation, however, when newspapers were lavishing praise on Andrew Mellon, certain cynics were pointing out that the former Treasury Secretary had never been of a particularly generous bent and that his reasons for founding the National Gallery were three-fold, none of which had anything to do with charity: to avoid estate taxes; to obtain a tax deduction of tens of millions of dollars; and to establish a memorial to himself.

In the same vein Paul's later donations of art could, in a real sense, be called not donations at all. Here is the method used by Paul's tax advisors when a painting is given away: the painting, perhaps purchased in 1936 for $500,000, is kept in Paul's home for thirty years, enjoyed by his family and friends, then is given to Yale or some other institution. The painting, the tax advisors would claim *and* prove (those called to testify to its value, the "experts"—usually art gallery curators dependent for a living on the "largesse" of rich people—are not likely to dispute its worth), the painting is now worth much more than $500,000. Thus is Paul able to enjoy a painting for three decades and then walk away with a large deduction from taxable income.

Paul's interest in art has not done much for art. The paintings he purchases are almost invariably those of artists long deceased. Artists living today, who could use some financial encouragement, get no such help.

Paul's taste in art was clearly evident by the mid-1940s. His first painting, bought when he was twenty-seven, was by the English painter George Stubbs, and depicted a horse named Pumpkin. "I didn't pay much for it," said Paul. "A few hundred pounds, I'd guess. I loved horses and that was the start of my passion for Stubbs."

Paul later paid twelve thousand pounds for a single painting by George Stubbs and acquired twenty-nine other works by that master.

Paul concentrated on the acquisition of seventeenth, eighteenth, and nineteenth century English paintings. He was fascinated, said *Fortune* magazine, with "the life and manners of the British landed aristocracy. . . ."

One of Paul's art agents explained his client's interest in English paintings: "He loved what they depicted. He loved the serene landscapes and the signs of peace and the order and the complete lack of conflict. The paintings made him nostalgic. He would like to have lived in that period."

Paul had a genuine fondness for art, a fondness that was also financially profitable. As the *Wall Street Journal,* January 3, 1967, revealed: "Art is a growth stock, a whopping tax deduction."

"The rise in prices," the *Journal* continued, "has led many purchasers to view art as an instrument whose growth potential puts many a high-flying stock to shame. According to dealers and others in the art world, some 'collectors' who not long ago thought Modigliani was some kind of Italian dish, now move in and out of the art market like so many Wall Street speculators, hunting bargains, and then trying to resell them at a fancy price."

Paul's spirited bidding for English art works drove prices up. As *Fortune* magazine, December, 1967, pointed out, in one decade the value of a Stubbs doubled. "It is," wryly remarked a less affluent collector, "difficult for the rich to lose money."

The way Paul collected paintings reflected the way he lived his life: expensively and out of the public eye. Invariably the art was purchased for him by an agent, though as he admitted he always looked at the painting a day or so before the sale or auction. The reason for using an agent was that his personal presence would undoubtedly drive the bidding up. Also, he considered it poor taste to flaunt his money by bidding for himself.

Foundations are another method the Mellons have used to avoid taxes. When Andrew Mellon died in August, 1937, it was revealed that he had left a huge sum to the A. W. Mellon Educational and Charitable Trust, under the trusteeship of Paul and David K. E. Bruce, irrevocably and perpetually, and to their self-designated successors. This of course left *control,* if not actual ownership, of the "donated" Mellon money in Mellon hands. It also left tax collectors in an ugly mood, as the *Herald Tribune,* August 29, 1937, pointed out: The gift "came at a time when officials of the United States Treasury . . . were expecting a windfall in taxes from the Mellon estate. So did the tax collectors in Harrisburg, where already eager functionaries had announced that the Mellon estate was expected to yield at least $28 million for the State of Pennsylvania."

Almost every foundation in the United States has come into being since the passage of estate tax and income tax laws. Incredibly, foundations are exempt from both income taxes *and* capital gains taxes. Either rich people suddenly became generous after the enactment of tax laws, or the foundations are clearly a way to avoid taxes. The latter is obviously the case.

One of the beauties of a foundation is that the money, tax free, is always available when needed.

But foundations were the furthest thing from Paul's mind in 1939 when the asthma his wife Mary Conover suffered from became worse. She thought her condition might be part psychological so Paul moved her and their baby daughter, Catherine (born 1937), to Zurich,

Switzerland, where she could be treated by the internationally famous Dr. Carl Gustav Jung.

Paul and Mary Conover spent six months in Zurich. They studied under Jung, carefully read each of his works, were immensely impressed whenever they had a chance to talk with the man who collaborated, and later broke, with Freud. Jung believed in the collective unconscious, that implanted in man's unconscious was a history of the human race. He was a pioneer in the field of psychoanalysis and possessed, Paul said, "one of the most extraordinarily fertile and profound minds of this century."

Paul finally became involved in the book publishing business his father had so firmly opposed. He and Mary paid the Pantheon Press to translate Dr. Jung's work into English. Later, through Pantheon, their book publishing efforts became more ambitious. "It was a way," Paul explained, "to publish important but commercially unfeasible works on a fairly large scale."

Paul also invested in a profitable area of publishing. He became a major stockholder in *Newsweek*.

Paul and Mary returned to the United States from Switzerland in May, 1940, and promptly donated the Woodland Road estate to the Pennsylvania College for Women (later renamed Chatham College). The donation doubled the physical size of the school and enabled it to greatly increase its enrollment. The mansion became an ultraluxurious dormitory.

The donation of the mansion Paul had lived in when he first went to work for the bank severed one of the last ties he felt bound him to Pittsburgh. Already he had resigned the directorships his father had bestowed on him. They had no appeal for him, no more appeal than the mansion.

Paul was determined to do positive things with the fortune his father left him, and few if any people in history have been in a position to do as much. Thanks to Andrew Mellon's cleverness in transferring his fortune before he died (he gave it to Paul and Ailsa), and also in setting up the A. W. Mellon Educational and Charitable Trust, practically no estate taxes at all were paid on the huge fortune. Paul, of course, became richer still as the corporations his father had owned continued to generate enormous profits.

The donations Paul would make through the years may have been partially motivated by a sense of guilt over where the money came from. Certainly he really did want to do positive things. He was like many rich people in this respect, however, in that the money he gave never hurt him: it was all tax deductible. Always the money was donated carefully, and never was more given than could be written off on taxes.

The same year, 1940, that Paul gave away the mansion on Woodland Road, he donated $55,000 to the Red Cross War Relief effort. In addition, his wife Mary gave $180,-000 to her alma mater, Vassar.

Paul did not want to work. Money was pouring in without any effort on his part. And even polo and fox hunting became boring after a while. He had the money to indulge any whim so, in the autumn of 1940, at age thirty-three, he enrolled as a freshman at the third oldest school in the United States, St. John's College in Annapolis, Maryland. He said he wanted to experiment with the "fundamental, old-fashioned methods of learning."

The program at St. John's was advanced, experimental, creative, a break out of the lockstep of American educational patterns.

109

Paul registered for four years at St. John's, but he stayed less than one. Under the St. John's program, students had to duplicate the experiments pioneering scientists used to test their discoveries. They also had to study the works of the first philosophers, from whose ideas other theories were developed. The St. John's course was based on the four-year study of one hundred books.

Why would a thirty-three-year-old man go back to school? A long-time observer of the Mellons offered an answer: "He was rich and he didn't have to make a living. A lot of people were saying, 'Sure, he's looked at a lot of pictures, and ridden some horses, but what does he really know?' The thing about Paul was that he wanted to understand. Maybe it's corny, but I think he wanted to get at the core of what life was, to participate in the human adventure.'

Paul's explanation for returning to school was that he wanted to "make up some important gaps" in his education. If so, he chose a good place to go. The St. John's teaching technique was invented by Robert Maynard Hutchins, president of the University of Chicago, and the four-year curriculum included the study of Augustine, Aquinas, François Villon, Machiavelli, Jefferson, Cicero, and Karl Marx. In astronomy students were required to construct and operate a model diopter, invented in the Third Century B.C. by Aristarchus to measure the sun, moon, and earth. Students also had to duplicate Harvey's blood circulation experiments by dissecting the heart of an ox.

Paul was searching for something, but he did not find it at St. John's. Soon he wearied of the routine, of rubbing shoulders with younger men, of living in a rented Eighteenth Century mansion near the college and com-

110

muting to the Upperville estate each weekend to be near Mary. So Paul did what would have horrified old Judge Mellon, who believed "less valuable" men should serve in the armed forces. In July, 1941, at age thirty-four, Paul volunteered for induction into the Army. Since the draft age had recently been lowered to twenty-seven, he had been in no danger of being inducted. Paul enlisted, close friends agree, because he had not found—in the past—what he was searching for. Maybe it was in the hurly-burly of army life.

Paul was inducted into the Army at Fort Lee, Virginia, and his basic training was probably the only time in his life that he had a degree of contact with average people. It did not wear well with him and after basic training he requested and was given an assignment in the cavalry. He graduated from Officers Candidate School as a second lieutenant in March, 1942, and served two years as a cavalry instructor, where his expertise at fox hunting and polo playing held him in good stead.

Wages were to a large extent frozen during World War II so Paul applied to the Fourth Regional War Labor Board to get permission to raise the wages of his servants at the Upperville estate. He came under the board's jurisdiction because he employed more than eight persons. The board gave its okay, saying Paul could give sixteen-cent-an-hour raises to servants he was presently paying twenty-four to forty-four and one-half cents an hour.

When it was revealed that one of the richest people in the country had been paying people twenty-four cents an hour, there was a wave of bitter wisecracks. Paul professed puzzlement over the comments, and he probably really was puzzled. He was a man who had isolated himself and his consciousness from a world beset with economic and other difficulties. He probably did not know that twenty-four cents an hour was a low wage for anyone to pay, much less a billionaire.

After two years as a cavalry instructor at Fort Riley, Paul was accepted into the Office of Special Services (OSS) and transferred to England. Oddly, the head of the OSS was William J. "Wild Bill" Donovan, who had headed a Justice Department investigation in 1925 that had absolved Alcoa of all charges in an important antitrust case.

The job of the OSS was to gather intelligence. In fact, the OSS was a forerunner of the CIA, and many of its members became CIA operatives. During World War II a number of wealthy Americans served in the OSS, including David Rockefeller, Allen Dulles, and David K. E. Bruce. One book, *Who's Who in the CIA*, which listed in telephone book fashion many alleged present-day CIA operatives and which reportedly shook that secret agency to its core, claimed that Paul was a CIA man as late as 1968. If the charge was true, he certainly was no behind-the-scenes thug dumping bodies into canals. More likely, since he was constantly entertaining heads of state and royalty, he probably gave informal briefings on his conversations to high CIA officials.

Paul also served in France during World War II. His superior officer was General George Patton, an old polo-playing friend.

That Paul was unaware of the difficulties of daily life was never more evident than in a remark he made when asked about his service in the OSS. "Junior officers," he said, "do a great deal of sitting around and waiting in a war. It's a good time for collecting one's thoughts."

The remark was amazingly insensitive; fifty million people would die in the war but Paul thought it was a good time to collect his thoughts. Still, his comment stemmed not from viciousness but from his self-imposed isolation. Perhaps as Gulf and other of his companies plunder entire nations, he simply is not aware of what is going on.

When the war was over Paul was a major. He probably deserved the rank since he had spent five years in the Army. Certainly he deserved the rank more than his first cousin Richard King Mellon deserved his. Richard King Mellon, Andrew Mellon's nephew and the man who would become most active overseeing the family billions, was commissioned a colonel almost the instant he joined the Army. He spent the war in the Pentagon and somehow was awarded the Distinguished Service Medal. Later he was made a lieutenant general.

In 1945, out of the Army, Paul continued to pursue his own lights. He lived at Upperville, with frequent trips to England. The Army had changed him not at all. He had not spent his time in the service meeting GIs; rather, he had hung around colonels and generals, people who entertained him and treated him as though *he* were the superior officer. The Mellon industrial and financial holdings represented raw power. *Ergo,* Paul was a powerful man.

The family businesses were prospering under the guidance of Richard King Mellon, no Andrew Mellon where finance was concerned but more than competent. *Fortune* magazine described what Richard King Mellon was doing shortly after the war: "In September, 1946, before most Pittsburghers were aware that he was back on the job, R. K. merged the Union Trust and the Mellon Bank into the Mellon National Bank & Trust Company. The result was a bank so big that its capital funds were the fifth largest in the U.S. and its deposits were fifteenth. ('My father and my uncle,' R. K. recalls, 'used to discuss such a consolidation every Christmas: but they never got around to it.') With the approval of his cousin Paul, R.K. became board chairman of the consolidated banks. . . .

"A few months before he consolidated the banks, R. K. merged the Mellon Securities Corporation and the Mellon Indemnity Corporation into two other companies . . . Mellon Securities was merged with First Boston Corporation, the nation's largest investment-banking house. . . . At the same time, the insurance company was sold to General Reinsurance Corp. for a 28 percent stock interest. First Boston, now the largest investment company in the world, has had an average after-tax return on capital of 12.5 percent annually for the past twenty years [1947–1967]. During the same period, the value of the Mellons' interest in General Reinsurance has gone up from $5.5 million to $60 million."

Sixty million in General Reinsurance alone! General Reinsurance is one of the "small" Mellon holdings.

The figures spinning in Richard King Mellon's head could not have been further from Paul's. "I have more money than anyone could ever need," he told a journalist. "My idea is to set about—sensibly—to do as much good as I can."

Paul's problem was twofold: the amount of good he could do was hindered by his own insistence that only donations that were tax deductible (and therefore really did not slow down the runaway stampede of his fortune at all) would be made; and, second, Paul was not really that sensible.

For example, Paul established the Bollingen Foundation. One of its purposes was to assist scholars in little-known fields of academic inquiry. Joseph C. Goulden in *The Money Givers* revealed that one of the Bollingen

Foundation grants was to study the work of Hugo von Hofmannsthal and "the origin and significance of the decorative types of medieval tombstones in Bosnia and Herzegovina."

This gift rankled Representative Wright Patman of Texas, Andrew Mellon's old nemesis and a believer that foundations should be taxed. "If the Mellons are more interested in medieval tombstones than in Pittsburgh poverty," said Patman, "that is the Mellons' affair. However, there is no obligation upon either the Congress or the American citizenry to give the Mellons tax-free dollars to finance their exotic interests."

Again, Paul saw nothing wrong in spending money on the study of tombstones in Bosnia and Herzegovina. He was interested, why weren't other people? He might have learned if he had pulled himself away from his horses and paintings. Paul not only set up the Bollingen Foundation but also devoted himself to running the Old Dominion Foundation, which he had set up in 1941. Old Dominion's philanthropies became truly impressive. During its first twenty-six years the Foundation gave away more than $47 million, to schools like Yale, Harvard, and St. John's, for cultural and environmental projects, and to individuals carrying on research.

Even these benevolences, however, failed to quiet Paul Mellon's critics. A Pittsburgh columnist complained that Yale and Harvard and St. John's were not the institutions most in need of assistance in this country, indeed that gifts of this sort only benefitted those already privileged.

It was true. Why not gifts to Iowa State? Or Platteville State? Or Butler? But Paul did not identify with schools like these, or with the students who attended them.

Paul did not listen to the carping of critics. He knew

that those who shared his interests and would appreciate his donations would be found at the prestigious eastern colleges and universities. He decided early not to be a populist or to try to drum up support for his philanthropies. The gifts were there—how they were there! —and he had not involved himself in the grubby financial maneuverings that provided for them.

An interview with newspapermen was rare for Paul. He preferred quiet seclusion. He never spoke out on politics, although in this area his contributions made crystal clear where his preferences were. In 1956 he was among several Mellons who donated $100,150 to Dwight Eisenhower's re-election. In 1968 he and his family gave at least $215,000 to Richard Nixon. This contribution, following right on the heels of President Nixon's "I will maintain it" statement regarding the oil depletion allowance, raised a number of eyebrows. Was Paul, despite popular belief, actively engaged in the running of Gulf? The answer was no, Paul was content to clip coupons and let others do the work. His donation to Mr. Nixon's campaign was probably more a reflex assumption that the Republican Party was best able to manage the affairs of the country. Nor was his donation to President Nixon's 1972 campaign likely to have been influenced by Mr. Nixon's "It should be increased" oil depletion allowance statement.

Tragedy struck Paul's life on October 11, 1946. At the Upperville estate, four hours after he and Mary had participated in a fox hunt, she suffered an asthmatic attack and died almost immediately. She was forty-one years old.

The former Mary Conover Brown, an intellectually brilliant woman, had enjoyed going to the races at Rolling Rock in Ligonier with her husband, had shared his interests in painting and book publishing, had blended perfectly into the stately life they had built together. Before passing away she had given Paul a second child, a son, Timothy, born June 22, 1942, while Paul was in the Army.

Paul remarried in May, 1948. His new bride was a recent divorcee, Mrs. Rachel Lambert Lloyd—"Bunny" to her friends—an heir to the Listerine fortune and herself the mother of two children. Bunny was a graduate of Foxcroft, a wealthy socialite ideally suited to be the wife of one of the world's richest men. She had no more idea how Gulf operated overseas than Paul did. And although it could be said that her husband quite literally owned the company, neither had much knowledge of its operations at home, either.

Eight

As American motorists waxed angry in long lines waiting to pay record prices to fill up their gas tanks in early 1974, Senator Henry Jackson of Washington conducted an inquiry into the "energy crisis." Senator Jackson's committee came up with facts that hardly were designed to bolster consumer confidence in the oil industry.

For one thing, where were the shortages? Oil companies, Senator Jackson pointed out, had more gasoline on hand at the end of 1973 than they had at the end of 1972. Why then, he asked, was there no gas available at the pumps? And what about profits? While motorists got into fist fights and independent truckers shot at one another, the big oil companies, led by none other than Paul Mellon's Gulf, were rolling in money: Gulf's fourth-quarter 1973 profits were up a phenomenal 91 percent over 1972 figures!

What was happening, it became clear, was that the super-rich oil corporations were holding the American people hostage until their ends had been accomplished. What the big companies wanted was the easing of environmental standards; the Alaskan pipeline; the elimination of competition from independents; and higher prices (meaning higher profits).

On March 22, 1974, President Richard Nixon called for the virtual suspension of the 1970 Clean Air Act. He also supported the repeal of offshore drilling restrictions, which would allow additional drilling on the continental shelf and which would further despoil remaining recreational areas. Score one point for the oil companies.

Congress caved in without a fight and cleared the Alaskan pipeline for construction. Score a double for the undefeated oil companies.

Said Brit Hume in the December 9, 1973, *The New York Times Magazine*: "The impact on independent marketers has been devastating. Hundreds of independent gasoline stations have shut down because of a lack of supply. Many that stayed open were forced to raise prices, wiping out their competitive edge." Score three points—a triple—for the oil companies.

Prices for gasoline and oil are at an all-time high in this country. So are oil company profits. Claiming there was a shortage, and talking about the "law" of supply and demand, the oil companies raised gasoline and oil prices to unprecedented levels. Score four points—a grand slam home run!—for the oil companies.

Even the Federal Trade Commission (FTC), no enemy of big business, has filed suit against the major oil companies. The FTC charged that the major oil companies "attempted to increase profits by restricting output." The FTC talked about "monopoly power" and "conspiracy" but, unfortunately, the average consumer is not likely to benefit soon, if ever, because of the suit. All the parties agree that the case will take years—perhaps decades—to litigate.

President Richard Nixon inaugurated his Project Independence in late 1973. Its purpose was to make the United States self-sufficient as far as its energy needs were concerned; in short, the U.S. would not have to depend on foreign sources in the critical area of fuel. No one familiar with U.S. oil companies had much hope that President Nixon's idea would succeed.

On March 20, 1974, the American Broadcasting Company did a special television report that studied the government's "attempts to regulate" and "influence" the oil industry. These attempts were broken down into four areas: one, depletion allowances; two, demand prorationing; three, foreign tax credits; four, import quotas.

All four government programs turned out to be fiascos.

The depletion allowance, as *The New York Times* has pointed out, is simply a scandalous tax dodge. Ostensibly passed to give the small wildcatter a break if his calculations about where oil is are wrong, it has been used by giants like Gulf (which knows when it drills a well that oil is most likely there) to avoid taxes.

Demand prorationing, as ABC revealed, was also self-defeating. This federal law was passed after the East Texas oil discoveries of the 1930s. These oil finds were so immense, and production of oil was so great, that the market was glutted. Oil was as cheap as dirt. To protect the economic interests of politically powerful families like the Mellons and Rockefellers, limits were set on how much oil could be pumped from a given well. The idea was to keep supplies down so that prices could be pushed to an artifically high level. And since there was a limit on how much could be pumped from a given well, oil companies were discouraged from discovering bonanzas like Spindletop.

Foreign tax credits also discourage domestic production. American oil companies are allowed to deduct any taxes they pay to foreign governments from their U.S. tax returns. They are allowed to do so not by a law passed by Congress, whose members are elected by the people, but by a special—and secret—ruling by the National Security Council! ABC News revealed that the National Security Council exempted U.S. oil companies from American taxes to encourage payment of taxes to Arab nations that it feared were leaning toward the Communists. Thus, the oil companies got a double break: they could take advantage of inexpensive drilling costs in the Middle East, and deduct from their taxes money paid to Arab governments.

Finally, import quotas. The amount of foreign oil that could be imported into the United States has been strictly held down by law. The U.S., although few people would know it from reading newspapers, is the Number One oil producer in the world: bigger than Iran, Kuwait, Saudi Arabia, Venezuela. The U.S., within its shores, produces more oil than any other nation. So import quotas were set up to restrict the amount of foreign oil that could be brought into the country: that foreign oil would compete with U.S. oil and drive prices down. Keeping prices and profits high, not giving the consumer a break, were the purposes of import quotas in the first place.

Senator Jackson revealed that there are more than 300 *billion* known barrels of oil still to be extracted from American territory, and that that amount is more than enough for many years to come. In addition, a parallel was drawn between meat prices and fuel prices. The skyrocketing cost of meat generated a nationwide consumer boycott in April, 1973, but, as with oil prices, the crisis did not ease until the big producers pushed their profits up to where they wanted them.

The energy crisis is not the first example of oil companies putting the squeeze on the American people. On January 28, 1969, five and a half miles from the shoreline of Santa Barbara, a high pressure oil drill gouged through a protective layer of rock holding back a huge reservoir of oil. "Withdrawing the drill," said the February 2, 1969, *New York Times*, "was like pulling a cork out of a bottle."

The subsequent destruction will never be fully known. Enormous reddish-brown clots of crude oil rapidly raced across a four-hundred-square-mile ocean area, at the same time splashing up on glittering white beaches where land was worth up to $2,000 a front foot. No longer were the beaches white, or the waters of the Pacific blue. Within hours thousands of birds were dead. So were millions of fish. One species of barracuda, indigenous to the waters off Santa Barbara, had 95 percent of its number suffer instantaneous death. Seal pups fell like bowling pins when they inhaled the poison.

More than two million gallons of oil spewed into the Pacific in the first ten and a half days after the spill.

On and on went the horror. On May 30, more than four months after the spill, one hundred barrels of oil a day continued to gush into the Pacific. Still no end was in sight as petroleum company engineers, so expert at extracting the oil, were unable to hold it back. At noon on the Sunday of the Labor Day weekend, not one swimmer could be found on Santa Barbara's East Beach, one of the most popular in all of California. But it was not over yet. Almost a year later the leak still had not been completely sealed.

The cause of the spill was the negligence of four companies operating an offshore oil rig in combination: Gulf, Union, Texaco, and Mobil.

The big loser was the city of Santa Barbara, whose proudest and most valuable asset is its beauty. The magnificent sand beaches overlook a spectacular blue ocean to lovely channel islands, two of which have been declared national monuments. The spill nearly crippled this quiet, clean city, dependent for its economy on fishing and tourism. Virtually no vacationers came to Santa Barbara in 1969. Scores of commercial fishermen were driven out of business. Simply cleaning up the oil-stained beaches cost $10 million. The loss of fish and wildlife was estimated at $50 million.

The city of Santa Barbara and the state of California sued the Federal Government (who had sold the oil leases) and the four oil companies for $1.06 billion. Private citizens who had their property damaged or ruined filed suit for an additional two billion dollars. The city and state also asked the court to enjoin the Federal Government from selling any more offshore California oil leases and to cancel the present leases. They contended that the oil companies contributed nothing to the state's economy, in fact that they were wrecking the economy. They also pointed out that even a minor earthquake, a not unlikely prospect in view of the San Andreas Fault, could precipitate oil spills that would paralyze the entire state.

Federal officials reacted with characteristic concern for the rights of the oil companies. Leases were not canceled and angry citizens organized mass demonstrations and ignited bonfires with petroleum company credit cards. The government then said it would consider holding public hearings before granting additional leases, though it made clear that present leases would not be tampered with.

This time it was the oil companies' turn to complain. Contending that "national defense" might be affected, Gulf vice-president E. L. Petree told *The New York Times* that "Gulf is concerned about the possibility that public hearings. . . may be unduly prolonged by enabling persons or organizations having no real or substantial interest in a proposed lease sale to unduly prevent leasing of the outer continental shelf."

This argument seemed reasonable to federal officials and soon oil lease sales were proceeding as before. Nor did the $1.06 billion suit brought by Santa Barbara and the state of California cause the oil companies any headaches. It was dismissed in January, 1972, and along with it went 342 counts of criminal pollution. The judge decided that the oil companies had "suffered sufficiently" from civil damage suits and publicity and fined each company a total of $500. The prosecutor called the decision "outrageous."

The Santa Barbara oil spill was the most destructive Gulf has ever been involved in, but it was far from the only one. In October, 1966, near Morgan City, Louisiana, a Gulf tanker capsized and 163,000 barrels of gasoline spilled overboard, staining the water and catching on fire. Six crewmen died in the blaze, a not unusual occurrence since working the big oil tankers is an extremely hazardous job.

But as mentioned, Gulf has little to fear from the government. On November 5, 1969, the company was sued by the Justice Department and charged with polluting New York waters. So badly have these waters been polluted by Gulf and others, in fact, that a lit match thrown in many of them can ignite a fire. Nevertheless, even if

Gulf were to lose the New York suit, the maximum fine by law would be $2,500.

There are reasons why the government is lenient toward Gulf. Back as early as the time of the original John Rockefeller, congressmen were "taken care of" by the oil men. Recently ABC News revealed that oilmen spent $500,000 sprucing up President Eisenhower's Gettysburg farm during the 1950s. In 1973 Gulf Oil pleaded guilty to making an illegal $100,000 contribution to President Nixon's 1972 campaign. No one, of course, received a prison term.

Leniency toward Gulf's attack on the environment is not the only way the government shows it is not hostile to the company, but often the average citizen has to look twice to learn the truth. On October 23, 1969, the Senate Finance Committee proudly announced it was cutting the depletion allowance from 27.5 percent to 23 percent. This was called a "victory" for the taxpayer even though the House of Representatives had earlier voted to cut the depletion allowance to 20 percent. No mention was made in the Senate Finance Committee that many people believe that there should be no depletion allowance whatever, that it is an out-and-out gift to the powerful oil companies.

The October 23, 1969, Senate Finance Committee action was in reality a victory for the oil companies because, as *The New York Times* revealed the very next day, a provision was added that "more than offset the reduction in the depletion allowance" for a number of companies.

Certain senators even voted to ignore the House Bill entirely and keep the depletion allowance at 27.5 percent. Included among these were oil millionaire Russell Long of Louisiana, Clinton P. Anderson of New Mexico, J. W. Fulbright of Arkansas, and self-styled populist Fred Harris of Oklahoma.

Voting to go along with the House cuts were Wallace Bennett of Utah, Carl Curtis of Nebraska, Paul Fannin of Arizona, and Clifford Hansen of Wyoming.

Principally responsible for altering the House Bill was Senator Russell Long, who remarked that, "We're entitled to have some fun, too."

In an editorial, October 24, 1969, *The New York Times* wrote about Senator Long's remark, asserting that he was maintaining "a tax loophole that has given him a tax-free income of over $300,000 in the last five years. To us it seems . . . an inexcusable instance of how a Congressional Committee Chairman may combine public service with private profit."

Nonetheless, on March 20, 1974, Frank Ikard, president of the American Petroleum Institute, told a national television audience that "I don't think the oil companies . . . have much influence."

Since Gulf's principal owner, Paul Mellon, used to pay his servants twenty-four cents an hour, it is not surprising that his company has failed to be progressive in the area of labor relations. In 1932 at the largest refinery in the world, Port Arthur, Texas, workers were paid twenty-five cents an hour, and in a way they were lucky to get it. Many of their fellows had been laid off without notice.

Things did not change much. On January 1, 1971, Gulf drivers had to come within minutes of a strike to obtain a thirty-five cents an hour raise. Gulf's profits after taxes the year previous had been $550.4 million.

Later, on May 29, 1971, drivers for Gulf and other companies who were picketing a Brooklyn oil terminal, became involved in an argument with nonunion drivers (who a number of New York reporters said were hired from the ranks of organized crime) and police broke up the picket line with clubs. Gulf's after-tax profits for 1971 were $561 million.

Gulf has gone into the real estate business in a big way. In the early 1960s the town of Reston, Virginia, was being billed as a model community. It was the lifelong dream about-to-become-reality of urban planner Robert Simon and was to have fountains and lakes and lovely bright apartments set in a futuristic pollution-free interracial community.

After a time there was a problem of financing, and in stepped Gulf with bags of money and what the *New Republic* called "the subtlety of a Latin American junta." Soon, as *The New York Times* pointed out, "one man's dream became a corporate subsidiary."

Robert Simon, who conceived the idea of Reston, was fired and replaced by a Gulf executive who began talking about "listening to the market" and "economic feasibility." The executive, Robert H. Ryan, said that many of Simon's ideas were ahead of their time. One of these was racial integration.

Robert H. Ryan was not the only corporate executive with a go-slow attitude on integration. Earlier, Simon had sought financing from General Electric, which also has ties with the Mellon family, and was turned down because one GE board member objected to blacks living in Reston, and other board members refused to override him. Gulf's man, Robert H. Ryan, agreed: "The American ethic for two hundred years has been for income levels to live with their own kind."

The *Wall Street Journal* was pleased, claiming that Reston was "about to be yanked abruptly back to earth," but the December 9, 1967, *New Republic* viewed the situation differently: "Most everyone else feels that Reston will soon be en-Gulfed in a mediocre urban sprawl, as was Radburn, New Jersey, the Greenbelt Towns of the New Deal and several other noble attempts to build good communities in this country."

The fears of General Electric and Gulf were not shared by the citizens of Reston. "They welcome the prospect of integration," reported *New Republic.*

Gulf has branched into dozens of activities having little connection with fuel. The company recently purchased Ringling Brothers and Barnum & Bailey Circus.

Gulf was the National Broadcasting Company's sole sponsor for the network's coverage of both the Republican and Democratic National Conventions in 1972. The cost of these telecasts ran into the tens of millions of dollars, but of course that cost was passed on to the consumer. Gulf won; it got its message across and stimulated sales. NBC won; it raked in millions. For the viewer watching television, however, there was only the opportunity to be misled: the commercials Gulf ran, if not patently breaking the law, certainly bent it. Anyone not knowing the history of Gulf Oil would have believed that the heirs of Anthony Luchich (the ads called him Lucas), who brought in the great Spindletop Gusher, owned the company. The truth, of course, is that Luchich was squeezed out of what is now a multibillion-dollar operation for $400,000.

Another advertisement had two service station attendants tossing clichés at a customer. "A penny saved is a penny earned," says one attendant. "Waste not, want not," advises the other. The banter goes on, trying to convince the viewer that he will save money buying Gulf gasoline. The fact is that Gulf, like other petroleum company giants—Standard, Shell, Texaco, Sunoco—has prices so nearly identical with its "competitors" that it stretches the imagination of even the most credulous to believe that some sort of price-fixing is not involved.

The oil companies, as Senator Jackson revealed, are in the process of carving up areas of the country for their own use. If Gulf is stronger than Texaco in a certain part of the U.S., Texaco may agree to pull out altogether. Gulf in turn would repay the favor by staying out of Texaco strongholds.

Ecologists, congressmen, public prosecutors, peace groups, labor unions, newspapermen, all have scored Gulf for one reason or another, but the unkindest cut of all had to be when the Ohio Conference of the United Church of Christ lambasted the company for everything from supporting the Portuguese wars in Angola, Mozambique, and Guinea Bissau to income tax evasion.

Gulf's president R. B. Dorsey retaliated by threatening to sue the church group for defamation of corporate character, but given additional time to think about the public relations of an international petroleum company taking a group of churchgoers to court, he wisely changed his mind.

The Reverend Reuben J. Schroer, a spokesman for the Ohio Conference, was disappointed. He wanted to go to court to prove the charges that had been made. He was not, however, surprised. The Reverend Schroer had predicted that the company would not want to produce in court tax reports "which would show that in 1968, for instance, Gulf paid less than one percent of its income in Federal taxes, less than taxpayers in the lowest income bracket."

In 1972, as *The New York Times* revealed, Gulf paid

less than two percent of its profits into U.S. Federal taxes. An interesting parallel could be made. One of the two largest single donors to Richard Nixon's 1972 campaign was Gulf stockholder Richard Mellon Scaife, who gave more than a million dollars.

Dr. Thomas Merton, director of the United Church of Christ's international relations office, gave another reason why R. B. Dorsey changed his mind about suing: "I don't think they would like to respond to a possible subpoena of the records of their African operations."

Dr. Merton could have added that Gulf would not like it known that, as reported in *Business Week,* May 2, 1970, it was the largest single foreign investor in Spain, whose government is headed by General Franco, a former supporter of Hitler.

Gulf Oil's support of right-wing governments should not be surprising. Andrew Mellon was an admirer of Benito Mussolini. "A strong man," said the Treasury Secretary in 1924, "has since come in to reestablish the Italian Government by Party and not by bargaining. Steps have been taken to abandon Government operation of the railroads and to cut taxes, and the budget this year will be practically balanced."

In 1926 Andrew Mellon's opinion of Mussolini had risen even higher: "Mussolini is making a new nation out of Italy. He is one of the world's most vigorous personalities. Many of his measures are unique indeed, but they are effective."

Andrew Mellon did more than just talk about the virtues of fascism, and therein lies one of the most sensational and least publicized stories of the 1930s. The Treasury Secretary contributed money to the Liberty League, an anti-black, anti-Semitic, pro-Ku Klux Klan organization that openly declared that the "New Deal is Communist" and that the "old line Americans [earning] $1,200 a year want a Hitler."

The Liberty League specialized in distributing a picture of Eleanor Roosevelt talking with two blacks, and warning of the "Jewish Brigade" President Roosevelt "had brought to Washington." But the Liberty League did more than propagandize, and the consequences could have been catastrophic had it not been for a great American patriot: retired Marine Major General Smedley D. Butler.

Smedley Butler was a Quaker who served thirty-three years with the Marine Corps and was the only living American to possess *two* Congressional Medals of Honor. It was fortunate for the nation that he did, for not many people with the story he had to relate would have been believed.

General Butler was approached by the Liberty League and "asked to organize 500,000 veterans into a Fascist army." The arms, Butler was told, would be provided by Remington. There was plenty of money to finance the operation, he was assured, and his prestige as a soldier would be invaluable in recruiting members of the American Legion to take part. Butler told the *New York Post,* November 20, 1934, in a story headlined "$3,000,-000 BID FOR FASCIST ARMY BARED": "The upshot of [the] proposition was that I was to head a soldier organization . . . in Washington [to] take over the functions of the government."

Smedley Butler went on to say that it was "explained to me that they had two other candidates for the position of 'man on the white horse.' He said that if I did not accept, an offer would be made to General Douglas MacArthur, chief of staff of the United States Army, whose term of office expires November 22, and that the third

131

choice would be Hanford MacNider, former commander of the American Legion."

General Butler told the Liberty Leaguers that the affair was treasonous, that he did not think ex-soldiers would follow either MacArthur or MacNider because both had opposed the veterans' bonus march. Butler then headed straight for Washington where he told the sordid story to the McCormack-Dickstein Congressional Committee. Here is part of the official report submitted to the House of Representatives by Congressman John McCormack of Massachusetts:

"This committee received evidence from Maj. Gen. Smedley D. Butler (retired), twice decorated by the Congress of the United States. He testified before the committee as to conversations with one Gerald C. MacGuire in which the latter is alleged to have suggested the formation of a fascist army under the leadership of General Butler (p. 8–114 D.C. 6 II).

"MacGuire denied this allegation under oath, but your committee was able to verify all the pertinent statements made by General Butler, with the exception of the direct statement suggesting the creation of the organization. This, however, was corroborated in the correspondence of MacGuire with his principal, Robert Sterling Clark of New York City, while MacGuire was abroad studying the various forms of veterans' organizations of Fascist character (p. 111 D.C. 6 II)."

How active was Andrew Mellon in the Liberty League, which quite literally plotted to overthrow the government of the United States?

The Lobby Investigation, headed by Senator Hugo Black, later a member of the U.S. Supreme Court, revealed that of the first $1 million the Liberty League received, $1,000 came from Andrew Mellon directly and an additional $60,752 came from relatives and executives working for his corporations.

In addition, George Seldes in *1,000 Americans* showed that Andrew and Richard Beatty Mellon gave the Sentinels of the Republic, a subsidiary of the Liberty League, $40,000 in 1936. This was two years *after* General Butler had testified that the League had tried to overthrow the government!

Andrew Mellon's involvement with the Liberty League was not uncovered until two years after Wright Patman's attempt to have him impeached was thwarted by his appointment as Ambassador to the Court of St. James.

Gulf does business in Spain with the fascist Franco. But the company does more than do business with fascist dictators, as might be expected from an organization that inherited the philosophy of Andrew Mellon.

Arnold Forster and Benjamin Epstein in their book *Danger on the Right,* published by the Anti-Defamation League of B'nai B'rith, revealed that in a recent five-year period Gulf gave $55,000 to the National Educational Program (NEP). The NEP, a tax exempt organization, sometimes employs John Birch Society members to produce its films. It also conducts Freedom Forums at which right-wing speakers extol the virtues of the open shop and racial segregation. One Freedom Forum speaker, William Grede, a former president of the National Association of Manufacturers, told a rally in Little Rock: "Industry has a moral obligation to make as much profit as it possibly can, and what business does with its profit is a moral matter which cannot be legislated by the government."

One of NEP's executives, George Stewart Benson, a rabid hard-line anti-Semite, has had nothing but praise for the Birch Society. Benson is opposed to Darwin's Theory of Evolution and says that a shorter workweek and higher pay is communistic.

Two other NEP leaders were Howard Bennett, a retired General Electric executive, and General W. P. Campbell, a member of the National Advisory Committee of Billy James Hargis's Christian Crusade. Campbell was also on the board of Americans for National Security and was a director of We, the People!

So Gulf Oil was as irresponsible at home as it was abroad. But it was making money. The company's assets grew more in the period between 1965 and 1970 (interestingly enough, Indochina war years) than they did in the previous sixty-four years of its existence: from some $4 billion in 1965 to more than $9 billion in 1970. By 1980 the company predicted, conservatively, that its assets would be more than $20 billion. *Twenty billion dollars!*

Gulf Oil's assets were greater than the Gross National Product of most countries. That did not seem unusual to Paul Mellon. Millions, billions, zillions, it was all *wonderful.*

Nine

PAUL GAVE A $1 MILLION DEBUTANTE PARTY ON JUNE 16, 1961, for his stepdaughter Eliza at the Upperville estate. According to *North American Newspaper Alliance* reporter Dorothy McCardle, it made the $280,000 party Henry Ford II threw the same week look like "a Sunday School outing."

A $1 million party was not Paul's style, and he was partly doing a favor for the ebullient Bunny; partly he was responding to the imperatives of his own social position. Paul, for all his withdrawal from the flossier aspects of jet set living, was still one of the nation's richest people. As such, he knew that a daughter's debut was the responsibility even the most reluctant parent had to assume without hesitation. That being the case, he decided to throw a party to end all parties: in good taste, of course.

Workmen erected a French pavilion to house the gathering and set up fifty tents—at a cost of $100,000—to put up overnight guests. Special roads were constructed so no one would get his shoes muddy in case it rained. Paul even had his dirt roads paved, but after the party had the pavement torn up so the estate would maintain its rustic atmosphere.

When the Duke and Duchess of Windsor visited America in the late 1960s, servants were assigned to flush the toilet for them. "That's the only thing," said a veteran of such social functions, "that Paul Mellon didn't provide."

There were seven hundred guests, including Bunny Mellon's close friend, Jacqueline Kennedy. President Kennedy wanted to attend but was prevented by his back injury.

The party began at 11 P.M. and lasted until dawn. The food was French and for atmosphere Paul had built Parisian sidewalk cafes and Gallic bars. It was as though the party was actually being held in France.

Paul even paid the expenses of two hundred wealthy college students to serve as escorts for Eliza's friends.

The party had something for everyone. There were two bands, Earl Coleman's and Count Basie's, and there were astrologers, a pianist, and a guitarist. Midway through the gala, Paul staged a forty-minute fireworks display over his man-made lake.

Wrote Dorothy McCardle: "Those who helped create the tent city and French pavilion said there had never been such a party in the United States."

Bunny was ecstatic. Fresh-faced, slender, Paul Mellon's second wife was delighted that her daughter Eliza had such a star-studded coming out.

Prior to his second marriage Paul had remained out of the social limelight. Bunny changed some of that. She enjoyed yachts and gay parties and elegant friends. Her closest friend was Jacqueline Kennedy who, after inheriting $10 million from the late president, married Aristotle Onassis. She married Onassis, a Washington columnist quipped, "because she felt like a little poor girl every time she had lunch with Bunny Mellon."

Even before she married Paul, Bunny had the sort of confidence the "established" rich possess. She was heir to the Listerine fortune and was utterly without financial cares. Jackie, on the other hand, was aware that the Bouvier fortune was as good as gone. Even her marriage to John Kennedy, and her subsequent inheritance, could not give her the same security as marriage to Andrew Mellon's only son.

Nonetheless, Jackie and Bunny were the best of friends, even though in many ways they were opposites. Bunny's great love was gardening, and she was perfectly happy spending days and weeks pursuing her interests. She was secure in her position, and in her money. Jackie was not. She was never sure there was quite enough.

After President Kennedy was inaugurated, Paul and Bunny donated a much sought after portrait of Thomas Jefferson by Rembrandt Peale to the White House. Bunny also talked her parents, the Gerard Lamberts of Princeton, into giving an 1819 portrait of Andrew Jackson to the White House. In addition, Paul and Bunny gave the President and Jacqueline two dozen bamboo-embossed vermiel bowls which Mary Van Rensselaer Thayer, author of *Jacqueline Kennedy, The White House Years,* described as one of the "more frivolous" gifts the First Family received.

The nation became acquainted with Bunny in 1961. Her friend Jackie named her to a twelve-member White House Committee to locate antique furniture for the executive mansion. On the committee were a number of people Bunny and Paul socialized with: Henry Francis DuPont, director of the Winterthur Corporation; Charles Francis Adams, great-great-great-grandson of John Adams, first president to live in the White House;

Mrs. Douglas Dillon, wife of the treasury secretary; Mrs. Charles W. Englehard, wife of a New Jersey industrialist; Mrs. Albert Lasker, a trustee of the Museum of Modern Art; John L. Loeb, the New York investment banker; and John Walker, director of the National Gallery of Art.

Bunny's real love was gardening, and Jackie put her in charge of caring for the White House Rose Garden. Jackie could not have made a better choice. Just as Paul ignored the outside world, lost in his studies of paintings, Bunny was totally involved in the world of plants. She had books on gardening dating back to the fourteenth century and, with trees and flowers from all over the world, had turned the Upperville estate into a botanist's delight.

Bunny was indeed Paul's wife. In an article for *Vogue* magazine, she bemoaned the fact that *alchemilla major* was "well known in England and, I think, not enough appreciated in America."

If that did not sound a chord with the American woman, she pushed on. She discussed *Ixia vividiflora, Platyclinis filiformis, Cymbidium miretta,* and the varieties of *Glendessary.*

Latin phrases aside, Jackie and Bunny considered the White House Rose Garden serious business. President Eisenhower had cut down the roses and turned the garden into a putting green. "It was awful," said Bunny.

Bunny really did know a lot about gardening. That did not mean that she did the work, any more than Paul's knowledge of paintings meant that he did his own bidding. When Bunny was put in charge of the Rose Garden, she brought two of her servants to Washington to make sure that her orders were carried out to the letter. By the time the garden was completed there were flowering trees and shrubs, a progression of different flowers that changed with the seasons, plus a careful selection of low-growing greenery of different shades, so that even during the pauses between blossoms the garden was vivid and colorful.

Bunny was in Antigua when President Kennedy was assassinated. She flew to Manhattan in a thunderstorm, landed at Idlewild, changed clothes in her New York apartment, and flew in one of Paul's private planes to Washington. There a limousine that belonged to Paul took her to the White House, where she was told that Jackie wanted her to arrange the flowers at the church, at the Capitol, and at Arlington.

When Bunny showed up at Capitol Hill she "was greeted," according to William Manchester in *The Death of a President,* "by a delegation: the director of the U.S. Botanic Gardens, an Army officer who had been placed under her command, and the president of the Allied Florist Association of Greater Washington. The first two delighted her, the third cheerfully informed her that every flower shop in the United States was remaining open this Sunday to accommodate people who wished to send bouquets here."

Bunny was worried about where all the flowers could be put. Finally she decided to store the flowers in one of the marble halls adjacent to the rotunda entrance.

After Lyndon Johnson moved into the White House Bunny completed the design of another White House Garden, the Jacqueline Kennedy Garden. This was done with the full approval of Mrs. Johnson, another friend of Bunny's, and there was a herb garden, cutting flowers, a grape arbor, crocus, tulips, candytuft, scilla hyacinths, osmanthus shrubs, and cherry and magnolia trees.

Bunny explained that the Jacqueline Kennedy Garden, the only section of the White House other than the Lincoln Room that is named for a former occupant, was designed with the views of George Washington in mind. Washington believed that a garden should be both beautiful and functional, and the garden that Bunny designed had a pool that shot water ten feet into the air, a croquet area that became a favorite of Lynda Bird and Lucy Bird, and a teak table where guests could sit while reading.

Bunny was honored for her work on the White House gardens by Secretary of the Interior Stewart Udall, who gave her the annual Conservation Service Award in 1966 for "outstanding efforts in furthering the conservation of natural resources."

If Bunny cared more for gardening than for people, the same could be said of Paul where paintings were concerned. And like Bunny, his interest brought him awards. In 1962 the National Institute of Arts and Letters gave him their Distinguished Service Award, an honor bestowed annually to an individual who excels in sponsoring and supporting art.

Paul may not have sponsored or supported art, but he kept art dealers happy. In 1958 he paid $616,000 for a Cezanne painting, "Boy in a Red Vest," the record price up to that time for a painting at auction. At the same time he paid $316,000 for Monet's famous street scene, "La Rue de Berne," and an additional $249,000 for another Monet, "Promenade."

Paul was not present at the auction, held at Sotheby's Gallery in London, but his agent said he had been authorized to make an "unlimited bid" for the Cezanne. Paul denied the statement, but not too vigorously. He simply did not want to risk his agent being recognized at future auctions and having prices bid out of sight by representatives of the seller.

There was speculation for a time over what Paul intended to do with his $616,000 Cezanne. Finally he revealed that he and Bunny had "wanted this picture very much" and that it was to be used for their "own enjoyment."

Thus a great masterpiece was kept from the public.

The same year Paul bought the Cezanne, 1958, he was given the Horace Marden Albright Scenic Preservation Medal for helping make Cape Hatteras part of the National Parks System. Paul had donated considerable amounts of money to beautify the area. Alexander Hamilton, great-great-grandson of the first Secretary of the Treasury, presented the award.

In 1960 Paul assumed two posts that usually would be considered important, but it was evident they were mainly honorary. All his life Paul had refused to be tied down by the drudgery of an office or to be directly involved in the cutthroat cynicism of master manipulations. There were other men more suited for it, and if he thought at all about the companies and what they did it was to hope they would generate increased dividends.

Regardless, Paul was elected in 1960, along with Westinghouse president Mark W. Cresap, Jr., and Koppers president Fred Foy, as a director of the Mellon National Bank & Trust Company. He was also named chairman and chief executive officer of the Mellon Institute, succeeding General Matthew B. Ridgway who had held the position since stepping down as Army Chief of Staff.

The two posts were completely honorary. Paul's advisors simply thought that on paper, anyway, it ought to look like he was doing *something*.

Paul spent little time on the business of the bank or the Mellon Institute. He spent even less time worrying about the activities of Alcoa, even though he was the company's major stockholder.

Ten

THE MINERAL FROM WHICH ALUMINUM COMES—BAUXITE
—comprises one-twelfth of the earth's surface, yet a
single company, Alcoa, held a one hundred percent monopoly on it in the United States for nearly fifty years.

The Mellons became interested in aluminum in 1889,
when approached by officers of the Pittsburgh Reduction
Company for credit. Aluminum, Andrew Mellon was
told, was one-third the weight of steel and just as strong.
It could have a hundred uses, a thousand, and all that
was needed was money. Through T. Mellon & Sons, Andrew provided $250,000 credit. In exchange he obtained
control of the company.

The first matter at hand was to eliminate competition.
The Cowles brothers had been producing aluminum in
Lockport, New York, for several years, but the Mellons
filed suit contending that a patent they owned had been
infringed upon. The Cowles brothers countered that the
patent had been stolen from them.

The case was heard in Cleveland, Ohio, before Federal Judge William Howard Taft. After a complicated

suit Taft found for the Mellons, a decision, as Harvey O'Connor pointed out, to be worth millions to the family. Now that the Cowles brothers were out of business, of course, the price of aluminum shot way up.

Other aluminum companies were formed but they had no chance against the determined Mellons. Those that would not merge with the Pittsburgh Reduction Company were bankrupted in fierce price wars. Meanwhile, the company went about buying up all land in the United States with known bauxite deposits containing forty or more percent alumina, the minimum needed to produce salable aluminum. Foreign competition was also eliminated in the United States, with a big assist from Andrew Mellon's friend Senator Cameron, by the passage of a fifteen-cents-a-pound tariff.

The Justice Department declared Alcoa a monopoly in 1912, finding, among other things, that Alcoa's only main competitor in the *world,* a German company, had signed the following agreement: Alcoa would not bid on aluminum contracts with the German government and the German company would not bid on American contracts; Alcoa and the German company would split fifty-fifty all sales in Africa, Asia, Australia, and other islands; Alcoa would take 25 percent of the European market and the Germans would receive 25 percent of the American.

Clearly, the world had been divided up by two companies, both of which could be counted on to vary not one cent in price on identical products.

The Justice Department brought other charges, too, but it was wasting its time. Even though Alcoa was found guilty of charging subsidiaries less for aluminum than was charged other companies, and of delaying shipments to competitors of its subsidiaries, and of furnishing competitors with material that was known to be defective,

143

and of squeezing out competitors by refusing to sell at all, Alcoa officials just smiled at the Justice Department decrees and continued business as usual. The company would promise to mend its ways, but it always slipped back into its old practices. And the laws lacked teeth. Most important, there was no competition, no company to keep Alcoa from doing whatever it wanted.

It would be difficult to go back through history and find a monopoly any more ruthless than Alcoa. Not only did it drive aluminum companies out of business, but other companies as well. If Alcoa had subsidiaries in the hardware business, and it did, it sold aluminum pots and pans to these companies at a cut rate, thus permitting them to undersell *their* competition. If the competition still remained in business, Alcoa would refuse to sell to it all. Where else could the competitor go?

A group of Frenchmen tried to challenge the Alcoa monopoly in 1912 and was promptly squashed. The French invested $5.5 million to get started and when they needed more money they went to Wall Street. No one, not J. P. Morgan, First National City, Chase, no one would loan the cash. In desperation they turned to Andrew Mellon who bought up their properties for $1 million less than they had paid for them.

Alcoa, like so many other large companies, really hit its stride during World War I. Aluminum was used for shells and shrapnel and machine guns and airplanes and tanks. It was no wonder Andrew Mellon so enthusiastically supported the war. He did not, however, support it sufficiently to suspend profits to help the Allies win. In fact, Alcoa charged the government 50 percent more for aluminum during the war than it charged the year after the war was over. Judge Mellon would have been proud that Andrew Mellon had not let patriotism get in the way of profits.

And those profits continued to roll in during the 1920s, primarily because the company could charge what it pleased. In 1921 Alcoa paid a dividend of 1,000 percent on original capital and in 1922, after the Fordney-McCumber Tariff Act had raised import taxes on aluminum 250 percent, the company paid a 500 percent dividend.

Life was not so pleasant for those who worked for Alcoa. The workday was twelve hours, often in blazing hot furnaces of rooms, and the pay was abysmally low. The company had a private police force and a network of spies to ferret out and discourage any tendency to complain. Employees who griped about conditions were summarily dismissed and denied work in the future. Those who discussed the possibility of organizing into a union were brutally beaten. Often employees were not even paid. Instead scrip was issued which could be used to buy food at company stores, and to pay rent in company housing.

In 1913 at a strike at the Alcoa plant in New Kensington, Pennsylvania, state police waded into picket lines and clubbed down workers.

In 1915 at Massena, New York, the state militia was called out to physically smash another Alcoa strike. One strike leader, Joseph Solunski, was bayoneted to death. Hundreds of workers were jailed, dozens beaten unmercifully. Charles Moritz, general manager of Alcoa's Massena mills, said that cheap labor could be imported from Canada. When the strike was finally beaten each state militiaman was given a set of aluminum cooking utensils by a grateful General Manager Moritz.

In 1916 in a strike at Alcoa mines in Arkansas a local union succeeded in obtaining wage increases from $1.75 a day to $2.00 a day. The company failed to live up to the agreement and the resulting strike was crushed by the importation of black and Mexican workers.

Alcoa's management was as creative in breaking strikes as it was in maintaining its monopoly. There was another strike at the Alcoa plant in New Kensington in 1916 and this was smashed when the company shifted its orders to other plants until the New Kensington workers agreed to management's terms.

The company played Divide and Conquer again in 1917 when a strike broke out at the East St. Louis plant, and this time the results were truly tragic. Management refused to listen to employee demands and instead went to Mississippi to urge blacks to come north. Ten thousand flocked to East St. Louis, where there were not nearly enough jobs. Angry white workers attacked the black strikebreakers and murdered at least twenty-five. Blacks were shot, hung from telephone poles, and beaten to death. Company property was kept safe from the rampaging whites by guards armed by E. M. Sorrels, who was later placed on Alcoa's payroll. A congressional committee subsequently placed blame for the massacre on Alcoa and other companies who had imported inexpensive black labor: "They pocketed their dividends without concern for their own workmen, black and white, who lived in hovels, the victims of poverty, disease, long hours and incessant labor."

Richard Beatty Mellon, in testimony before the Senate Committee on Interstate Commerce, March 23, 1928, was asked if he approved of private police toting machine guns at the Mellon mines. "It is necessary," he said. "You could not run without them."

146

Senator Burton Wheeler, during the same committee investigation, asked Richard Beatty Mellon if he had seen any of the miners to talk over problems with them. "No," answered Richard Beatty. "I did not go to see them. I would not be out there, way out in the mines."

Alcoa and the other Mellon companies evinced a curious attitude towards workers. Because cheaper labor could always be imported to smash strikes it showed the "depravity" of workers. In addition, management felt the twelve-hour day was desirable because it exhausted employees and kept them out of saloons. Rotten living conditions, went management's reasoning, proved the employees did not want anything better.

Meanwhile, the Justice Department continued to make unenthusiastic gestures at breaking up Alcoa. The Federal Trade Commission filed monopoly complaints against the company in 1928 and 1930, but Andrew Mellon was still a powerhouse in Washington and not much was going to come of FTC grumblings. Even in 1937, when the Government filed suit in earnest to break the monopoly, Alcoa still had years of appeals to exhaust before there would be competition.

One suit that might have come to something never got off the ground, thanks, many thought, to Andrew Mellon. Attorney General Harlan F. Stone was only days away from bringing an antitrust action against Alcoa when Coolidge suddenly elevated him to the Supreme Court. Many Washington observers thought they detected the long arm of the Secretary of the Treasury in the convenient removal of Attorney General Stone, especially since his successor never followed up on the charge.

Alcoa hardly became more progressive in its employee relations during the 1930s (it was estimated that between 1934 and 1936 alone the company spent $400,000 on industrial spies) , but a more dangerous aspect of the company's policies was revealed on December 11, 1944, when Senator George Aiken of Vermont read into the Congressional Record the report of the Power Authority of the State of New York which said that the cartel agreement Alcoa had with the Nazis "had the effect of limiting the production of strategic light metals in the United States."

Drew Pearson was more specific: "The monopoly between Aluminum Company of America and I. G. Farben kept magnesium away from the American aircraft industry and retarded our production of planes."

A number of people claimed that the Alcoa-I. G. Farben cartel agreement helped prolong the war. In any event, the simple revelation that Alcoa was making secret deals with the Nazis was shocking enough. I. G. Farben, Hitler's largest financial backer, conducted numerous experiments with chemicals and drugs, using concentration camp inmates as guinea pigs. In one case I. G. Farben bought 150 women from the Auschwitz camp for seventy dollars apiece "in contemplation of experiments of a new soporific drug." A Farben memo noted: "Received the order of 150 women. Despite their emaciated condition, they were found satisfactory . . . the tests were made. All subjects died. We shall contact you shortly on the subject of a new load."

Alcoa was big in defense contracting in World War II, but in the postwar years it would grow bigger still. By 1969, *Business Week,* in its issue of May 10 of that year, pointed out that, "The most vigorous promotor of aluminum powder metallurgy today is the Aluminum Co. of America. It accounts for a huge portion of the current 250-million-lb. annual market for aluminum powder. Some 75% of that volume, it is estimated, goes into bombs for the Vietnam war."

Alcoa's aluminum is also used to "scale down" the size of the hydrogen bomb to make it "controllable."

Alcoa finally began to experience "competition" toward the end of World War II when the Reynolds Metals Company, with government backing, got into the aluminum business. After the war Kaiser entered the field. Both companies were able to break into the market by purchasing or leasing plants constructed by the government.

Still, there was no real competition. Alcoa set prices and the others followed. Often not one penny difference existed among what the companies were charging for the same product. Whenever Alcoa announced a rate boost, the others faithfully followed. They could do little else. Decades of monopoly had left Alcoa with the best men and the most money, materials, know-how, customers, credit, and capacity. Alcoa slowed down not a stride when up against Kaiser and Reynolds. For example, in 1958 the company shipped 35 percent more aluminum abroad in a recession year than it had in the Korean War boom year of 1950.

It was obvious there was no competition. Mellon National Bank & Trust Company loaned money to the Kaiser auto company. The Mellon Bank was a bond trustee in 1953 for a $29-million Kaiser Aluminum stock issue.

During the early 1950s Alcoa sponsored Edward R. Murrow's controversial television program, *See It Now.* Alexander Kendrick, author of *Prime Time,* a biography of Murrow, explained the benefits of such a sponsorship: "The Aluminum Company of America's association with *See It Now* had, in ways that only Madison Avenue could calculate, changed its popular image from that of a virtual monopoly constantly being pursued by the Government, into one of public service."

Murrow scored Senator Joseph McCarthy for the witchhunts on *See It Now*. McCarthy retaliated against Alcoa, as described by Kendrick: "The Senator himself sent a telegram attacking Alcoa directors if they intended to continue using 'tax money' to sustain Murrow, meaning money spent on institutional advertising instead of going for taxes. Implied, as usual, was an investigation of some sort. Alcoa wavered but finally stood firm. A year later, however, it would drop its sponsorship of *See It Now* in another controversial situation, though the ostensible reason would be to sell 'pots and pans' instead of mere good will."

"Sometimes," Edward R. Murrow remarked in thundering understatement, "there is a clash between the public interest and the corporate interest."

Today the company has greater electric power capacity than the countries of Australia, Brazil (with a population of 100 million people), or Spain. As late as 1955, according to the *American Bureau of Metal Statistics Year Book,* Alcoa had cornered—not counting the Communist countries—48 percent of the world's aluminum-producing capacity.

And Alcoa was branching out, the way a conglomerate should, with only token interference from the government. One minor aggravation occurred in 1964 when the Supreme Court forced it to divest itself of the Rome Cable Corporation. The purchase violated the Clayton Anti-Trust Law, since both companies were manufacturing the same products.

Alcoa began producing an almost countless variety of goods, including violins, period furniture, apartment buildings, coating for spark plugs, pop-top cans ("selling like free money," said *Business Week*), home siding, outdoor telephone booths, irrigation pipe, curtain walls, door frames, awnings, balconies, foil insulation, railings, Venetian blinds, acoustical ceilings, conduits, and ducts.

In the early 1960s Alcoa went into the real estate business in a big way. "Of course," Alcoa executive vice-president Leon E. Hickman told a journalist, "we're in business to make money and our stockholders should fire us if we don't. But if we want our company to survive as a private enterprise, we can't stop there. We must do things which the average American, who fears Big Business, will consider a service to him and to our country."

One of Alcoa's housing projects, Century City in Los Angeles, had apartments which started for the average American at $400 a month, rising to the $4,000 a month Jack Benny paid.

Alcoa went into other real estate projects: United Nations Plaza, New York City; James Whitcomb Riley Center, Indianapolis; Allegheny Center, Pittsburgh; Kips Bay Plaza, New York City; Lincoln Towers, New York City; Park West Village, New York City; Society Hill, Philadelphia; Washington Plaza, Pittsburgh; and Golden Gateway, San Francisco.

Despite Leon Hickman's assertion that Alcoa wanted to provide a service for average Americans, the real reason the company went into real estate was to avoid taxes. The depreciation of real estate, at least on paper, can be very high. Alcoa deducts the depreciation of the apartment complexes from its aluminum profits. As *Business Week* put it, "Alcoa figures the cash drain on a company in its position is about half what it would be for a developer with no other business."

Alcoa has again entered into agreements that look suspiciously like cartels. It has formed a partnership with Britain's Imperial Chemical Industries, Ltd., to sell aluminum throughout Europe. It has also formed a partnership with the huge Furukawa Electric Company of Japan, and with Montecani in Italy.

The Vietnam War was good to Alcoa. The company is a major defense contractor and its assets—$1,463,752,-348 in 1963— had more than doubled by the end of 1972.

Alcoa, like Gulf Oil, is in many foreign countries, including Brazil, Venezuela, Mexico, and India. Said *Business Week*: "If these markets [referring only to Western Europe] grow one-quarter as far and as fast as the U.S. market, the future will be simply too big and too busy to be believed."

Eleven

PAUL MADE ONE OF HIS MORE CREATIVE DONATIONS IN 1962. It was a trailer fifty-two feet long and inside the trailer was an art gallery twelve and one-half feet high and ten feet wide. The gift was presented to the Virginia Museum of Fine Arts and was billed as the "biggest display vehicle in the world." Its purpose was to travel throughout Virginia so people could view the Mellon art collection.

On the trailer's maiden trip, which followed a lavish dinner Paul hosted at the Upperville estate, the mobile art gallery was packed with millions of dollars of portraits, including works by Delacroix, Gauguin, Cezanne, and Manet. The paintings were guarded only by the driver because, as Washington columnist Betty Beale revealed, "there is so much secret built-in protection it is considered foolproof."

Columnist Betty Beale described the scene: "Equipped with a music system, a soundtrack describing the paintings, a book stall at one end, drop canopies and panels for literature on the outer sides, and a drop stairway, the whole to-do is worked by pushbuttons and cost over $500,000."

Paul proudly predicted at the dinner he gave that the trailer would be traveling continually for at least ten years, and perhaps for as long as twenty.

As Paul's former secretary revealed, Paul and Bunny had a "mutual toleration" for each other's hobbies. In short, they stayed out of each other's way. Often they vacationed separately even though, as one New York reporter put it, "Paul's whole life has been a vacation."

Paul squirreled himself away for weeks at a time working on the cataloguing of his art collection. The fragile Bunny spent her days directing an array of servants hired specifically to help with her gardens.

For Paul, his life had meaning. He had successfully avoided the trap Andrew Mellon had set for him, and he had more money than his father ever had. Also, Paul was becoming as famous collecting paintings as Andrew Mellon had been, and there was none of the ugly publicity his father had reaped. Paul believed that is the way it should be; he was not hurting anyone; if Gulf and Alcoa were, that was the fault of the companies, not something that should reflect on him.

Paul's art expertise was rewarded on January 30, 1963, when he was named president of the National Gallery of Art. Actually, he had held the position briefly earlier, when the Gallery was first opened, but at that time he was appointed more in recognition of Andrew Mellon's donation than for recognition of his knowledge of the masters.

In March, 1964, Paul donated four paintings, described by *Newsweek* as "priceless," to the National Gallery of Art, with the specific proviso that they hang in the United States Embassy in Great Britain. The paintings, two each by Canaletto and Arthur Davis, dated as far back as 1754. John Walker, director of the National Gallery (and therefore an employee of Paul), praised the gift: "For years, embassies of foreign nations in Washington have had works of art from their own national collections. It is my hope that Mr. Mellon's patriotic gift will inspire other American donors to contribute in this way toward the decoration of our embassies abroad."

Paul's donation may have been patriotic, but it did not help large numbers of people to see the great art work.

In March, 1966, Paul decided to give the National Gallery a twenty-fifth anniversary birthday present (the Gallery was officially opened in 1941) and this time the public did get a chance to view a portion of the magnificent private collection he had accumulated.

The paintings he loaned (his present was a loan, not a gift) to the National Gallery for six weeks filled twelve rooms and included sixteen Boudins, nine Monets, four Cezannes, fifteen Degas, twelve Renoirs, six Gauguins, six Van Goghs, sixteen Bonnards, twenty-three Vuilliards, eleven Seurats, plus works by Corot and Picasso.

When he announced the loan of the paintings, Paul said, "Six months ago we had no such idea, but John Walker, our director, persuaded us. I admit it makes a nice exhibition. I haven't seen all the pictures together this way before. I think they help to make a nice birthday party."

A journalist asked Paul why the impressionist painters appealed to him. "That's a horrible question," he answered. "But let's see. It's a feeling. Like the name of the style. There is an ever-fresh impression of seeing. Looking at a picture day after day in my home, I feel as if I see new things. The paintings help me to see things in real life that I wouldn't otherwise notice."

Paul hesitated a moment, then told the journalist: "That's not why I collect, but in a room a picture is a new dimension, and I enjoy a walk in the country more because I've seen so many of these pictures."

Maybe so. But among the things the paintings evidently did not help him to notice, or at least that he never spoke about, was the Indochina War, the Gulf-sponsored wars in Angola and Mozambique, and Alcoa cartel agreements that kept prices artificially high.

The night before Paul's paintings went on exhibition for six weeks, he gave a private dinner party at the Solgrave Club in Washington, D.C., for 110 guests, including Mrs. Lyndon Johnson, Vice-President Hubert Humphrey, Chief Justice Earl Warren, Mr. and Mrs. Winthrop Aldrich, and Mr. and Mrs. Thomas Gates.

After the dinner Paul gave a rare speech. "It is very embarrassing," he began, "for a collector to be caught with his paintings down."

Paul continued: "The pride of ownership of paintings is typified to me by a recent cartoon in the comic strip 'Peanuts.' Snoopy, the dog, was on top of his doghouse, and voices were wafted up to him through the door. After other remarks, one of the voices says: 'Look over there—I'll bet that's something you never expected to see,' and another voice says: 'Fantastic!', after which Snoopy says: 'I can always tell when they have come to see my Van Gogh.'

"But since I'm never sure of this pronunciation, I've made up a little limerick to cover my embarrassment:

"I'll never, with confidence, know
If Van Gogh is Van Gock or Van Go

I admit, to my shame
This chameleon name
Makes my highbrows feel terribly low.

But a friend of mine said 'Off the cuff
One might say that his name was Van Guff'.
But, regardless, I fear,
What he did to his ear
Was playing a little too rough."

Just about the time Paul was delivering his poem at
the Solgrave Club, a bloody *coup* was just ending in
Southeast Asia, a *coup* so bloody, in fact, that conservative
estimates list the number of dead at 400,000. Paul probably was unaware the coup was occurring, since virtually
nothing has been written about it in this country, either
during or after. Few people know it even took place,
fewer still know that one of its principal beneficiaries was
Alcoa.

Twelve

UNTIL 1949 INDONESIA HAD BEEN A COLONY FOR 350 YEARS, first under the Portuguese, then under the Dutch, briefly under Great Britain (1811–1916) , then under the Dutch again, for a short time under the Japanese (1942–1945), and back again to the Dutch until independence. What had started as the spice trade under the Portuguese soon became, under the direction of the more enterprising Dutch East India Company, a looter's paradise. Sugar, tea, coffee, and indigo were harvested by the natives and sold on world markets by the Dutch.

On August 17, 1945, after the defeat of the Japanese in World War II, a popular nationalist revolutionary named Sukarno proclaimed the Republic of Indonesia independent, and the people of the country rallied to him. The reasons were obvious: in 1945 Indonesia had about 100 million people, was rated as the fifth richest nation in the world in natural resources, was blessed with extremely fertile land and rich deposits of oil, tin, and bauxite, yet this sixth largest country on earth was 93 percent illiterate and had a *per capita* income of eighty-two dollars a year.

Indonesia was eloquent evidence of the evils that 350 years of colonial domination bring. In 1945 there was *one* university, two university professors, ten agricultural experts, less than one hundred engineers, and just over one hundred doctors.

With the Japanese defeated, the Dutch thought that the three thousand islands that comprise Indonesia were once again rightfully theirs; Sukarno did not think so and for the next four years the poorly-equipped peasants fought a war of liberation against 110,000 Dutch troops. Finally, at the Round Table Conference at The Hague in 1949, Sukarno won independence for his people.

Conditions improved under President Sukarno. For one thing, Indonesians regained their self-esteem; no longer was there the fear that a Dutch or Japanese officer would decide to strike citizens in the face with a rifle butt for "lack of respect." Another improvement was the hospitals that were built. People who had never seen a doctor before were now receiving medical attention. Income rose. Inroads were being made toward abolishing illiteracy.

Sukarno made errors. He was so imbued with a hatred of colonialism that he adopted a foreign policy opposed to any U.S. presence in Asia. Worse, although not a Communist himself, he lifted the Dutch ban outlawing the Communist Party.

From the moment the ban was lifted, United States policy-makers decided that Sukarno had to go. Mainland China was already Communist, Indochina was headed that way, all Asia was in turmoil. The thought of more than 100 million Indonesians jumping off the Capitalist Ship dried the throats of State Department planners. The CIA—minus Kermit Roosevelt—was called on to duplicate its Iranian triumph.

In their book *The Invisible Government,* Washington

correspondents Thomas Ross and David Wise described the CIA's first attempt to topple Sukarno. After equipping a small air force with B-26 bombers to fly support missions to aid anti-Sukarno, pro-United States insurrectionists, the CIA sat back to wait for victory.

It did not happen, at least not in 1958, during the first attempt. In fact, an American pilot, Lawrence Pope, was shot down and captured. Authors Ross and Wise explained what happened:

"Three weeks before Pope was shot down, Dwight D. Eisenhower had emphatically denied charges that the United States was supporting the rebellion against President Sukarno.

" 'Our policy,' he said at a press conference on April 30, 'is one of careful neutrality and proper deportment all the way through so as not to be taking sides where it is none of our business.

" 'Now on the other hand, every rebellion that I have ever heard of has its soldiers of fortune. . . .'

"But Pope was no freebooting soldier of fortune. He was flying for the CIA, which was secretly supporting the rebels who were trying to overthrow Sukarno."

President Eisenhower never bothered to contradict this assertion, nor did anyone else. They would have looked silly if they had tried. When Sukarno visited President Kennedy in the United States, Kennedy told an aide: "No wonder Sukarno doesn't like us very much. He had to sit down with people who tried to overthrow him."

Arthur Schlesinger, Jr., in his bestselling book *A Thousand Days,* confirmed the CIA's role in the attempted *coup* of 1958: "His (Sukarno's) deep mistrust of the white west was understandably compounded in the case of the United States by his knowledge that in 1958 the CIA had participated in an effort to overthrow him."

Finally, if additional proof were needed, *The New York Times,* April 25, 1966, had this to say: "In Indonesia in the same year (1958), against the advice of American diplomats, the CIA was authorized to fly supplies from Taiwan and the Philippines to aid army officers rebelling against President Sukarno in Sumatra and Java. An American pilot was shot down on a bombing mission and was released only at the insistent urging of the Kennedy Administration in 1962. Mr. Sukarno, naturally enough, drew the obvious conclusions. . . ."

But the CIA did not stop trying to overthrow Sukarno, and by September, 1965, a full-scale insurrection—a better word would be bloodbath—was underway in Indonesia. Said *Time* magazine, December 17, 1965: "Communists, red sympathizers, and their families are being massacred by the thousands. Backlands army units are reported to have executed thousands of Communists after interrogation in remote jails. Armed with wide-bladed knives called 'parrangs,' Moslem bands crept at night into the homes of Communists, killing entire families and burying the bodies in shallow graves. The murder campaign became so brazen in parts of rural East Java, that Moslem bands placed the heads of victims on poles and paraded them through villages. The killings have been on such a scale that the disposal of the corpses has created a serious sanitation problem in East Java and Northern Sumatra where the humid air bears the reek of decaying flesh. Travelers from these areas tell of small rivers and streams that have been literally clogged with bodies. River transportation has at places been seriously impeded."

The Guardian of Great Britain, April 7, 1966, carried this account: "Estimates of the total number of Indonesians killed in political massacres after the attempted coup [the excuse for the massacres, an excuse bought in its entirety by the western press, including *The Guardian,* was that the pro-United States Indonesian generals were trying to protect Sukarno from a Communist takeover, but this was proven patently false when the generals arrested Sukarno and his entire cabinet and set up a military dictatorship] of September 30 are being revised as fuller information comes in from outer regions. One western ambassador considers 300,000 to be a conservative estimate, and other compilations run far higher.

"A traveller who knows the island of Bali well, and speaks the language . . . describes mass executions and the annihilation of village after village in some areas. A consular official in Surabaja accepts a figure of 200,000 for Bali, which has a population of 2 million.

"Estimates of the dead in Sumatra also range around 200,000 and a similar figure for Java is generally regarded on the low side. When the death tolls for other islands such as Borneo and Sulawesi are added, the total may well be upwards of 600,000. Just how many of these are Communists is another question.

"It appears certain that the great majority of the dead were innocent victims of political hysteria. . . .

"In some areas, Communist suspects were shot or poisoned, but usually the Moslem youth beheaded its victims with the parrang. . . . The heads were often impaled on fences and gateposts. . . .

"Rivers in many parts of the country were clogged with corpses for weeks. A European resident of Surabaja described finding bodies washed up by the river on to his back garden."

The May 8, 1966, *New York Times* quoted an Indonesian schoolteacher from a village near Jogjakarta: "My students went right out with the army. They pointed out

P.K.I. (Communist Party) members. The army shot them on the spot along with their whole family; women, children. It was horrible. . . ."

Who was responsible for the overthrow of the popular Sukarno and the imposition of a military dictatorship? In the June 19, 1966, *New York Times,* James Reston wrote: "One of the most persistent complaints among officials in Washington is that our political troubles in Vietnam are not balanced adequately by reports in the press of the more hopeful political developments elsewhere in Asia.

"The savage transformation of Indonesia from a pro-Chinese policy under Sukarno to a defiantly anti-Communist policy under General Suharto is, of course, the most important of these developments. Washington is careful not to claim any credit for this change in the sixth most populous and one of the richest nations in the world, but this does not mean that Washington had nothing to do with it.

"There was a great deal more contact between the anti-Communist forces in that country and at least one very high official in Washington before and during the Indonesian massacre than is generally realized. General Suharto's forces, at times severely short of food and munitions, have been getting aid from here through various third countries, and it is doubtful if the coup would ever have been attempted without the American show of strength in Vietnam or been sustained without the clandestine aid it has received indirectly from here."

Max Frankel, also writing in *The New York Times,* began his article by saying that "The Johnson Administration found it difficult to hide its delight with the news from Indonesia. . . ."

Alex Campbell, managing editor of the *New Republic,*

visited Indonesia in 1969 and then described what life was like under the military dictatorship: "The government plans to send some 60,000 (prisoners) to forced labor on rubber plantations in Borneo. Perhaps 10,000 have already gone there. They are said to be dying like flies. Meanwhile those still in the camps may be slowly dying of starvation. . . ."

Campbell continued: "All Indonesians have to carry identification cards about race, religion and occupation. The cards of the relatives of political detainees bear in addition a warning that they are suspected of having Communist sympathies. This usually means that they are refused jobs, or that they soon lose the jobs they have. . . . The punishment of the children is to be refused admission to schools. . . . Meanwhile, new suspects continue to be arrested and put in prison or otherwise disposed of."

Campbell devoted a good deal of time to describing the wretched living conditions of the people, then dwelt on the life-style of one General Sutowo: "His daughter's costly wedding was the talk of Djakarta in March. It continued for days, there were thousands of guests, and the general had closed-circuit television installed into his huge home, as the only way by which he could watch the entire proceedings. The father of the groom artlessly exclaimed, 'I did not realize my son was marrying a princess!' "

Incidentally, President Sukarno's home was turned into a Holiday Inn.

According to a 1966 article in *Suara Pemuda Indonesia,* an Indonesian newspaper, prior to the military coup that toppled Sukarno, the United States had equipped forty-three army battalions which were under the leadership of reactionary generals. In addition, between 1956 and 1959, more than two hundred high-ranking officers were trained in the United States.

But the real tipoff as to who overthrew Sukarno came during the 1967 Fulbright Committee Hearings on the U. S. Foreign Assistance Program:

Senator Sparkman: I want to go back to. . . . our continuing military aid to Indonesia. At a time when Indonesia was kicking up pretty badly—when we were getting a lot of criticism for continuing military aid—at that time we could not say what that military aid was for. Is it secret any more?

Secretary McNamara: I think in retrospect, that the aid was well-justified.

Senator Sparkman: You think it paid dividends?

Secretary McNamara: I do, sir.

It is true that the motives of the United States in helping topple Sukarno were mostly political, that this country feared the effects of another anti-American country in the same part of the world as Mainland China. But, as so often happens, national interests and corporate interests were one and the same.

In January, 1967, the military dictatorship passed a Foreign Investment Law which, among other things, guaranteed United States investors against all losses due to "war, revolution or insurrection."

A month later, on February 19, 1967, the narrator of an NBC documentary put it another way: "The New Order wants Goodyear back. They, like dozens of other foreign capitalists, are anxious to return because the wealth is there—not just rubber, but oil, tin, lumber, spices, almost everything."

One of the greatest beneficiaries of the Indonesian *coup* was Alcoa, as pointed out by the Associated Press in March of 1969: "The agreement (between Alcoa and the generals) provides for one of the biggest single investments in Indonesia outside of long-term oil operations."

The truth is that much of Indonesia is so rich in bauxite that Alcoa plans an *initial* investment of $100 million for exploration and equipment. Of course, most Alcoa stockholders, counting a cornucopia of dividends reaped from the new Indonesian investments, will remain unaware that none of it would have been possible had not at least 400,000 human beings died.

Thirteen

Paul was honored in London on January 16, 1965, when the Royal Society of Arts awarded him the Benjamin Franklin Medal for "Anglo-American understanding," in recognition of his prowess as a collector of British paintings and as a gesture of gratitude for a gift he had made earlier: in 1960 he had presented his portion of John Locke's personal library to the Bodleian Library in Oxford. The collection contained eight hundred volumes and eleven manuscripts, including the seventeenth-century philosopher's extensive weather diary.

The award ceremony was held at Buckingham Palace and the Franklin Medal was presented by Prince Philip, president of the Royal Society of Arts.

Paul was a personal friend of Prince Philip. He and Bunny had entertained the Prince and Queen Elizabeth at the Upperville estate in October, 1957. It was the only private home the royal couple visited on their tour of America. Bunny insured that her orange and yellow dahlias and her pink and blue michaelmas would provide a blaze of color by covering them with cotton cloth for weeks before the visit. The Queen and Prince Philip looked with approval at Paul's best yearling thoroughbreds, then after a leisurely tea took off from Paul's private airstrip in the British Embassy's plane.

Having royalty fly to your house for tea is a true ego builder, but for Paul it was simply further proof that he had lived his life successfully. He had become like the idle English aristocracy he had so long admired.

Two months before the Queen's visit, in August, 1957, Paul gave his only daughter, Catherine Conover Mellon, in marriage to John William Warner, Jr. Catherine had graduated from her stepmother's school, Foxcroft, and made her debut at a 1955 dance in Upperville. Her fiance, John Warner, was an assistant United States attorney at the time of the marriage, but better posts were ahead. He became assistant secretary of the navy and in 1972 secretary of the navy. No public official mentioned that there might be a conflict of interest, what with the U.S. Navy being one of the world's largest purchasers of oil and its secretary being married into the Gulf Oil fortune.

Today John Warner, thanks to an appointment from President Nixon, is head of the 1976 Bicentennial Commission.

The year Paul won the Franklin Medal, 1965, he built a house at 125 East 70th Street in Manhattan. The house was only the third or fourth built from the ground up in Manhattan since World War II and, said the *Pittsburgh Press,* "As such, it is respected and admired by architects, realtors and home lovers who didn't think it could be done on this overcrowded island, where real estate prices are astronomical."

The house was five stories high and the bottom two were reserved almost exclusively for servant quarters and kitchens. The house had an elevator, which the *Pittsburgh Press* called an "essential adjunct," and it was completely air conditioned. The house had a bar, a flower room, a dumb-waiter, an art storage room, a laundry, a clothes-pressing room, seven baths, five lavatories, two kitchens, and fourteen other rooms. Bunny's bedroom was 17′ x 18′ while Paul's was only 16′ x 15′.

The *World Telegram,* which did not believe the house was particularly large, called its construction "a rare and wonderful thing." Still, the newspaper sympathized with Bunny and Paul: "If the Mellons want to give a big party in New York, they will have to hire a hall like everybody else."

Perhaps the furnishings in the Mellon house can best be appreciated by the fact that when Jacqueline Kennedy gave a lavish party for former Pakistani President Mohammed Ayub Khan, she borrowed Bunny's furniture.

The house, which was estimated to have cost about $1 million, and which Bunny and Paul intended to use only on visits to New York, was assessed for tax purposes at $200,000. The $200,000 evaluation might seem low to some people, but it must have struck Paul as exceedingly high. In September, 1972, for example, one estate in Westmoreland County, Pennsylvania, owned by relatives of Paul, was given a property tax assessment of $4,300, despite the fact that it consisted of 106.7 acres and was purchased originally for $280,000. Charlesworth, another Mellon family estate in Westmoreland County, consisted of 481 acres and was assigned a 1973 property tax evaluation of $4,800. Chief County Tax Assessor Robert Elston was fired for "incompetence" after he objected to the low assessment. Elston had been on the job for four and one-half years.

Paul was above such petty squabbles. He was too busy

buying up paintings. His collection came to include Titian's *Toilet of Venus,* Van Eyck's *Annunciation,* and Raphael's *Madonna and the House of Alba.* Said John Walker, the director of the National Gallery, after Paul purchased twenty-one masterpieces at one time: "It was the greatest private collecting *coup* in our country, perhaps of all time."

Paul was indeed the art collector *par excellence.* Three of the paintings he loaned to the National Gallery for its twenty-fifth anniversary were Monet's *On the Cliffs, Madame Monet and Her Son Jean,* which Paul acquired for $515,340; Cezanne's *Boy in a Red Vest,* which cost $616,000; and another Cezanne, *House in Provence,* with an $800,000 price tag.

Paul described the thrill of buying paintings: "The great sense of triumph, plus the sleepless night before."

Some people worry about being unemployed. Or their sons having to die in wars. Paul's concern was different: "I remember particularly," Paul wrote in the *Washington Post,* "a most beautiful large Boudin. I will never forget it; I dream about it; I covet it still. But it is irretrievable."

Paul became involved in collecting other treasures besides paintings. He paid $23,520 for a two-and-a-half ton Seventeenth Century statue of King William III, which he shipped from Great Britain to his estate in Upperville. He also purchased a musical manuscript which had been written in 1470 for the court of Charles the Bold and consisted of fifty-seven compositions in five languages. The manuscript was quite literally priceless. The composition that most fascinated Paul, *L'Homme Arme,* had been sought for a century.

Paul's ingenuity knew no bounds. He managed to acquire a copy of Blake's epic poem "Jerusalem," which the poet had illustrated himself. He also purchased the first work ever printed in the English language, *Recuy-ell and Historyes of Troye,* and the first illustrated English-language book, *Myrrour of the Worlde,* both of which were produced in the Fifteenth Century by William Caxton.

In August, 1966, Bunny and Paul threw another of their patented parties, this time in Cape Cod. The occasion was Jacqueline Kennedy's birthday. A special tent was erected for dancing, and for some reason never explained to the American taxpayer a White House aide was flown in to make sure everything ran smoothly.

On hand for the party were Secretary of Defense Robert McNamara, Douglas Dillon, Katherine Graham, Arthur Schlesinger, Jock Whitney, Kenneth Galbraith, William Paley, and the hairdresser Kenneth, who set himself up next to the ladies' room in case any of the women needed emergency work on their hair. Said columnist Mary O'Hara: "Mrs. Paul Mellon and Jacqueline Kennedy have a lot in common: exquisite taste, beautiful manners, and the wit to attract and keep as friends some of the smartest people in the world."

Bunny and Jackie did have a lot in common. As a former Mellon employee put it, "Both are concerned with their own well-being, and nothing else. They spend a lot of time admiring themselves in a mirror."

It is also debatable whether Robert McNamara, for example, is one of the "smartest" people in the world. His predictions of imminent victory in Indochina did not bring calls from Las Vegas that he replace Nick the Greek as the nation's oddsmaker.

Nevertheless, the party was quite proper. White-jacketed waiters carried trays of drinks to tuxedoed guests who spoke in hushed monotones. The atmosphere was not corner bar. Although the party was in Cape Cod, it was strictly *Upper*ville.

Upperville it was on May 14, 1968, when Paul hosted a wedding for his stepdaughter Eliza. The groom was Viscount Moore, the only son of the eleventh Earl of Drogheda of Parkside House, Englefield Green, Surrey, England. The viscount, whose real name was Henry Dermot Ponsonby, proved he was "just folks" by insisting that he be called "Derry."

Five choir boys from the Washington National Cathedral were brought to Upperville to sing during the ceremony. Guests who had come from New York to Dulles International Airport were chauffeured to the wedding in a pair of chartered buses. Other guests arrived in Cadillacs and Rolls Royces.

Jacqueline Kennedy was at the wedding, along with her daughter Caroline, who tossed daisies into the aisle in front of the bride. Other guests included David K. E. Bruce's second wife, Evangeline, Mr. and Mrs. Hugh Auchincloss, and Joseph Alsop. After the wedding ceremony, as had become Paul's trademark, a large tent was set up and three hundred persons began dancing to rock and roll music played by Bill Harrington and his orchestra. The music jangled the nerves of the aristocratic Bunny and she told the orchestra to tone it down.

It was a blueblood marriage. Eliza, besides being tied to the Mellon billions, was the granddaughter of Gerard Barnes Lambert who built the Listerine mouthwash fortune and then made even more with the Gillette Safety Razor Company. Eliza traced her roots all the way back to Thomas Lloyd, deputy governor under William Penn.

The bridegroom, Henry Dermot Ponsonby (Derry), was the son of the managing editor of the *Financial Times,* Ltd., chairman of International Trade Fairs,

Ltd., Governor of the Royal Ballet, a director of the *Economist* Newspaper, Ltd., and a director of the Financial and Provincial Publicity Company.

The wedding was simply one example of the sort of entertaining Bunny and Paul do when rich friends are invited. The parties are different when other people come. For example, Bunny was hostess for 250 members of the Herbs Society of America: "They were wonderful. I didn't see one unhappy face, though they had to see the gardens in the rain. We made them box lunches, chicken salad, cottage cheese with herbs and cucumber, and water cress, ham and curry sandwiches. Of course, we had to have lots of herbs."

Another time Bunny was the hostess for 150 members of the New York Horticultural Society. On still a different occasion it was eighty veterinarians, who came to see Paul's horses and ate their lunch in the stables.

The Upperville estate has a museum, swimming pool, tennis court, huge gardens, plant house, guest house, summer house, and a schoolhouse (Paul inherited Andrew Mellon's distrust of public education) where the children received special tutoring. One of those children, Stacey Lloyd III, was decorated by the State Department for his work as a foreign service officer in Laos.

Bunny summed up her life at Upperville: "This is the way I really like to live. With this peace."

But how was life in Pittsburgh? Bunny and Paul did not live there, yet what they owned dictated conditions for more than half a million people.

Fourteen

THE ECONOMY OF PITTSBURGH IS DOMINATED BY THE Mellon National Bank & Trust Company, and the domination goes far beyond the fact that 52.1 percent of all commercial bank deposits in the Pittsburgh metropolitan area are concentrated in its coffers. It is a psychological domination as well as a financial domination. A visitor to downtown Pittsburgh cannot walk two blocks without running into one of the bank's branches. He cannot long turn on a radio or television or open a newspaper without being told of the bank's services. He cannot drive the freeways without reading about the bank on billboards.

A July 8, 1967 (the statistics would be even more startling today), staff report prepared for a subcommittee of the Committee on Banking and Currency of the U.S. House of Representatives revealed some eye-opening facts: of the $10.5 billion in bank trust assets in the Pittsburgh metropolitan area, the Mellon Bank had 72.3 percent of the total; the Mellon Bank had 89.4 percent of all employee benefit account assets; and, most important, the

Mellon Bank had invested 73.2 percent of all the money it held in trust in stocks.

The House subcommittee that compiled the report estimated that holding 5 percent of the stock in a major corporation usually assured minority control over that corporation because opposition views were unlikely to be able to muster that large a bloc of votes (few stockholders actually exercise their right to vote).

The subcommittee revealed that the Mellon National Bank & Trust Company, through its combined trust departments, held 6.6 percent of the common stock of National Steel Corporation; 5.1 percent of Allegheny Ludlum Steel; 15.1 percent of Pittsburgh Auto Equipment Company; 5.6 percent of TRW, Inc.; 7.8 percent of Mesta Machine Company; 9.1 percent (preferred) of Reichhold Chemicals, Inc.; 14 percent of Diamond Alkali Company; 15.2 percent of Nalco Chemical Company; 18.5 percent of Koppers; 33.4 percent of Daily News Publishing Company, McKeesport, Pa.; 25.3 percent of Fisher Scientific Company; 47.3 percent of Bush Terminal Company; 99.9 percent (preferred) of First Boston Corporation; 5.9 percent of Armstrong Cork Company; 5.7 percent (preferred) of Apollo Industries; 17.1 percent of Gulf Oil; 31.3 percent of H. J. Heinz Company; 13.5 percent (common) and 24.6 percent (preferred) of Mine Safety Appliances Company; 11.7 percent of Harbison-Walker Refractories Company; 6.5 percent of National Union Life Insurance Company; 23.5 percent of General Reinsurance Company; 14.4 percent (preferred) of Flintkote Company; 19.8 percent (preferred) of Certain-teed Products Corporation; 25.3 percent (common) and 15 percent (preferred) of Aluminum Company of America; 7.9 percent of Mirro Aluminum; 8.3 percent of Central Hudson Gas & Electric

Corporation; 5.2 percent (preferred) of Pacific Lighting Corporation; 21 percent (preferred) of Montana Dakota Utilities Company; 13 percent of North Penn Gas Company; and 5.5 percent of Idaho Power Company.

It is clear from a look at the trust holdings of the Mellon Bank that Paul's power extends far beyond the first chapter analysis of the holdings of Gulf, Alcoa, Carborundum, Koppers, and a superficial look at the bank itself. In addition, most of the companies the Mellon Bank controls, themselves control a wide variety of affiliates and subsidiaries. The list would be staggering.

But the Mellon Bank is more powerful still. The uses of interlocking directorates (directors of the Mellon Bank who also sit on the boards of other corporations) is another method of exercising control over some of America's most powerful businesses. Men who sit on the board of directors of the Mellon Bank are also directors (when the Mellon Bank has more than one director on another company's board it will be indicated) of the following corporations: United States Steel; Jones & Laughlin Steel (2); Armco Steel; Crucible Steel; Allegheny Ludlum Steel (3); Granite City Steel; Latrobe Steel (2); Firth Sterling; Vulcan Mold Iron Company; Screw & Bolt Corporation of America; General Steel Industries, Inc.; Westinghouse Airbrake Company (2); Pullman, Inc.; TRW, Inc.; McKay Machine Company; Blaw-Knox Company (2); H. K. Porter Company (3); General Electric; Westinghouse Electric (2); Diamond Alkali Company (2); Koppers (2); International Minerals & Chemicals Corporation; Union Carbide; Daily News Publishing Company, McKeesport, Pa. (2); Hanna Mining (2); Youngstown Steel Door Company; Pennsylvania Railroad (2); Fisher Scientific Company (2); Consolidation Coal Company (3); Gulf Oil (4);

H. J. Heinz Company (4) ; Mine Safety Appliances Company (2); Brockway Glass Company; Jeannette Glass Company; Pittsburgh Plate Glass Company (3); Harbison-Walker Refractories Company; Metropolitan Life Insurance Company; National Union Fire Insurance Company (2); Aluminum Company of America (3); Titanium Metals; Pennsylvania Power and Light; Bell Telephone Company of Pennsylvania (2); Duquesne Light Company (2); Columbia Gas Systems, Inc.; Monongahela Power Company of Ohio (4); R. J. Reynolds Tobacco Company; National Lead Company; Coleman Company, Inc.; H. H. Robertson Company; James H. Matthews Company; Elwin G. Smith & Company, Inc.; National Cash Register Company; AVM Corporation; General Motors Corporation; Chrysler Corporation; Eaton, Yale & Towne, Inc.; Packwell Standard Corporation (2); Martin-Marietta Corporation; Rockwell Manufacturing Company; Eastman Kodak Company; National Casket Company, Inc.; Pittsburgh Lake Erie Rail Road Company; Cleveland & Pittsburgh Rail Road Company; Pittsburgh, Fort Wayne & Chicago Rail Road Company; Great Atlantic & Pacific Tea Company, Inc.; Tiffany & Company; Oakland Consolidated Corporation; Pennsylvania Company (2); and General Atronics Corporation.

The House subcommittee report pointed out one of the obvious dangers of so many interlocks: "The Mellon National Bank has director and/or stockholder links with four major chemical companies which to some extent compete with each other. Similarly, Mellon has the same sort of ties with twelve steel companies. Such arrangements clearly have the potential of seriously restraining competition."

The situation is fraught with danger for the American

consumer. How can a director of the Mellon Bank who knows the bank owns 5.1 percent of Allegheny Ludlum Steel also sit on the board of U.S. Steel? If such a director is trying to help U.S. Steel take away Allegheny's business—as he should be doing as a director of the company—how can he in good conscience pretend to serve the interests of the Mellon Bank, which very much should want Allegheny Ludlum to capture a portion of U.S. Steel's business so Allegheny Ludlum can prosper?

Also, the Mellon Bank has interlocking directorates with both General Electric and Westinghouse. In the early 1960s these two companies were convicted of price fixing and it was estimated that the American public over a period of years had been overcharged hundreds of millions of dollars. A number of General Electric executives went to jail because of the price-fixing. Did Westinghouse and General Electric make secret deals to maintain steep prices because the people in charge of each company realized they had no real reason to be competitors at all? Was the price-fixing because of interlocking directorates like the one the Mellon Bank maintains, where the bank interlocks with both Westinghouse and General Electric?

The House subcommittee report summed up how powerful the Mellon National Bank & Trust Company is: "It is clear from this examination that not only is the commercial and trust side of banking in the Pittsburgh metropolitan area dominated by one huge banking institution (Mellon Bank) and one medium-sized banking institution (Pittsburgh National Bank), but the entire economy of the area is greatly influenced, and perhaps even controlled, by these two banks through various interlocking relationships with the leading corporations in the area. The effect of this situation spreads far beyond the Pittsburgh area alone, because many of these corporations are nationally, and even internationally, important in their fields."

Despite his reluctance, art collector Paul Mellon did indeed influence the world. The money, which he wanted to use but he did not want to earn, made certain of that.

Fifteen

In his old age, Paul began to appreciate his ancestors.
How narrow-minded could Judge Mellon have been?
Surely the judge must have had a vision: why else could
Paul live such an enjoyable life? And Andrew Mellon.
Paul figured he must have been wrong to dislike his
father. Had not the money for his wonderful philanthro-
pies come from Andrew Mellon?

Paul was moved by nostalgia. He organized a family
reunion in June, 1968, in Northern Ireland to commem-
orate the 150th anniversary of Thomas Mellon's coming
to America. Some fifty Mellons, including Ailsa, Paul,
and Richard King, got together on the original homestead, which only a few weeks before had been a pigsty.
The family had spent $250,000 to renovate it and to erect
a monument to Judge Mellon.

The Mellons were treated like visiting royalty in
Northern Ireland. Ulster Prime Minister Terence
O'Neill observed that more than one-quarter of the oc-
cupants of the White House had come from Scotch-Irish
ancestry, along with such famous Americans as J. Paul

Getty, Davy Crockett, Horace Greeley, and Sam Houston.

The Ulster Government arranged accommodations for the Mellons at plush hotels and picked up the tab for fifteen limousines the family rented at $7.20 an hour. The government also paid for a black tie dinner at the Parliament Building. Northern Ireland newspapers called the family "The Mighty Mellons." It was never revealed why the Northern Ireland Government, hardly one of the world's wealthiest, felt it should pay bills for the fabulously rich Mellons.

Bunny and Paul are used to the good life. They have homes in Washington, D.C., New York City, Cape Cod, and Antigua, but their first love is the stone house at Upperville. The home is as much the work of Bunny as anyone. It stands about a mile off a dusty farm road into which bumps have been built to slow down speeders, and its color was described by *New York Times* writer Sarah Booth Conroy as "no color." Bunny was pleased with the description: "Nothing should stand out. It all should give the feeling of calm. When you go away you should remember only the peace."

Bunny, who often refers to her husband as "Mr. Mellon," discussed her home and her life at Upperville: "Mr. Mellon and I meet on art and books. He has such a wonderful light sense of humor. He's really such fun to be with. He writes clever bits of poetry and teases me all the time. I like it."

Bunny was in a talkative mood. She chatted about her friend Jacqueline Onassis. "When all that William Manchester business was happening, Jacqueline Kennedy was serenely pasting these pictures of Jack Kennedy in the book (a scrapbook Jackie had given Bunny) for me."

Bunny went on: "Jacqueline was an old and true and

loyal friend of mine a long time before she went into the White House. I can't say anything but good of her. People see only the clothes but don't really see her. Her marriage? Just right for her, I'm sure. Aristotle Onassis is a wonderful man. So intelligent. And so charming."

Bunny discussed another friend, Lady Bird Johnson. "I don't think Mrs. Johnson was ever properly appreciated. I really liked her. She is so straightforward. She would say, 'Now I know my colors are dreadful.' One time I was at the White House when they had tied fake chrysanthemums to plants, and she came up to me and said, 'Isn't it awful?' "

Bunny talked about Patricia Nixon. "Of course I would be happy to help Mrs. Nixon, but she hasn't asked me. I am a Democrat. My husband teases me about it all the time. But gardens aren't political. I tell my husband, 'Trees have to be watered whether the Administration is Republican or Democratic.' "

Bunny's remarks may not have been profound, but she was an ideal wife for Paul. Her husband, "Mr. Mellon" as she calls him, occasionally returns to Pittsburgh, not to become involved in the running of family businesses but to receive briefings on how his investments are doing. Often these briefings were given by Nathan W. Pearson, a sixty-two-year-old businessman who was Paul's personal representative on the boards of Gulf, Alcoa, Koppers, and Carborundum. More often than not Paul and Nathan Pearson met in Paul's private offices on the thirty-ninth floor of the Mellon Bank building, private offices which other Pittsburgh businessmen call "heaven."

There is even a church, Mellon Presbyterian, named after the family, in Pittsburgh. Citizens of Pittsburgh refer to it as "Mellon's Fire Escape."

Paul prefers to avoid Pittsburgh, where the family name is hardly popular. In fact, when he is seen in public at all it is usually at a race track. His Rokeby Stables have become almost synonymous with great thoroughbred horses.

On June 5, 1964, his horse Quadrangle won the Belmont Stakes, the one-and-a-half mile "Test of Champions." Quadrangle defeated such outstanding thoroughbreds as Roman Brother, Hill Rise, and Northern Dancer (who had won the Kentucky Derby and Preakness and was going for the "Third Jewel" in racing's Triple Crown).

Arts and Letters, named for the society that presented him an award for art collecting, was named Horse of the Year in the U.S. in 1969. The next year, 1970, Paul was named as the country's outstanding thoroughbred breeder by the New York Turf Club. In one race alone in 1970, Paul's Run the Gauntlet captured the Garden State Stakes and first prize of $211,392.

Rokeby Stables' Fort Marcy has twice won the prestigious Washington, D.C., International at Laurel, but perhaps Paul's greatest horse was Mill Reef, who raced exclusively in Europe. In 1971 Mill Reef took France's Prix d'la Arc de Triomphe and a purse of $187,000. For the year Mill Reef earned $610,000, with victories in the Epsom Derby, the Eclipse Stakes, the King George VI Stakes, and the Queen Elizabeth Stakes. Mill Reef was voted Horse of the Year in Europe, and Paul was voted Owner of the Year.

Paul's horses won three of the four major races at Saratoga in 1972, an unprecedented feat. Key to the Mint won the Whitney and Travers, and Summer Guest took the Alabama. Key to the Mint ran against Secretariat in 1973 but was defeated.

Paul has spent most of his life out of the public eye. *The New York Times,* May 2, 1971, pointed out one of the reasons: "One characteristic the family shares is an intense craving for privacy. In several weeks of research, not one Mellon or relative of the family agreed to be interviewed. Moreover, some business and financial associates of the family, when informed by Mellon spokesmen that a story on family activities was unwelcome, closed the door to information about family business or foundation matters.

"The Mellons, with their great wealth, are shielded by unlisted telephone numbers, phalanxes of lawyers, business and financial counselors and family retainers. . . .

"This is by design, however. In fact, so great is the desire for anonymity that one branch of the family a few years ago hired a public relations agency to keep its name out of the papers. Furthermore, the very thought of articles tying together the family fortune makes Mellon lawyers uneasy."

And well it might. It would be in order to take a look at part of that fortune, to see what the lawyers and the family are afraid the public might learn.

Sixteen

THE DEATH OF AILSA MELLON IN AUGUST, 1969, AND THE reading of her will brought into sharp focus once again the fact that in order to tie the Mellon fortune together it is necessary to look not only at personal family holdings like Gulf Oil and Alcoa, but also at the enormous financial influence the Mellons wield through tax-free foundations, foundations which, incidentally, own large blocks of stock and are used to control entire corporations. At the time of her death Ailsa Mellon was undoubtedly, as *The New York Times* and *Fortune* magazine pointed out, the richest woman in the world, and one bequest alone was $363 million to the Andrew W. Mellon Foundation. This "gift" effectively took the money out of the domain of the tax collector and kept it under family control, particularly under Paul's control, where it could be used, among other purposes, to vote the Mellon interests in stockholder fights. So great is the power of just three of the Mellon foundations that they totaled, in 1969, assets of almost $1 billion. These three foundations are:

	1969 Assets	1970 Grants Paid
Andrew W. Mellon Foundation	$697 million	$29.9 million
Sarah Mellon Scaife Foundation	$169 million	$ 3.8 million
Richard King Mellon Foundation	$110 million	$ 4.6 million
	$976 million	$38.3 million

Even a brief analysis of these figures reveals that Paul and his relatives are not as generous as their publicity men and their cheerleaders among the ranks of the press would have people believe. Actually, donations amount to only about 3 percent of total assets and even invested at banks at low interest rates the money would earn more than that. Thus the Mellons do not even pay out what profits the foundations make, much less giving anything away. The foundations are tax dodges which concentrate corporate control in the family's hands.

Another way to grasp what is almost ungraspable—that is, the vastness of Mellon holdings—is to consider that on March 29, 1974, the Dow Jones Industrial Average of thirty leading industrials stood at 846.68. Here is what the Dow Jones Average would have been if it had been compiled from some of the companies the Mellons either have an interest in or control:

	Company	March 29, 1974 Closing Price
1.	Gulf Oil	22⅞
2.	Alcoa	47
3.	Carborundum	40¼
4.	Koppers	51
5.	Westinghouse Electric	20½
6.	Allegheny Ludlum Steel	31⅛

	Company	March 29, 1974 Closing Price
7.	United States Steel	42½
8.	General Electric	54¼
9.	National Steel	33⅛
10.	Eastman Kodak	106⅛
11.	Pittsburgh Plate Glass Company	26¼
12.	Chrysler Corporation	17⅝
13.	General Motors	49⅜
14.	Jones & Laughlin Steel	19¼
15.	Pullman	63
16.	Montana Dakota Utilities	31¼
17.	Martin-Marietta	17
18.	Greater Atlantic & Pacific Tea Company	13
19.	Certain-Teed Products	17¾
20.	Warner Lambert	36
21.	National Cash Register	36¾
22.	H. J. Heinz	46¼
23.	Union Carbide	37
24.	Armstrong Cork	27
25.	Reichhold Chemicals	9⅝
26.	Pacific Lighting	20⅝
27.	TRW	19⅜
28.	Hanna Mining	33
29.	Columbia Gas	25⅝
30.	Brockway Glass	12⅛

1,006⅝

Seventeen

PAUL WAS HOSTING ANOTHER DINNER PARTY, THIS ONE TO honor the trustees of the nation's two centennial museums—Metropolitan and Boston. "We wish the museum further long, long life," he said, "many decades of peaceful acquisition, continuous future freedom from interference by the cities, states, the Federal Government, the artists, the minorities, the hippies, and many happy returns of this centennial year."

It was a Saturday night and Paul talked to a journalist after the dinner. He was unhappy, he said, because he had not been able to go on his usual fox hunt that morning. It turned out that he had to write a speech he was to deliver in a few days in York, England, to celebrate the 200th anniversary of the Gimcrack Stakes.

And so it went. Perhaps Paul should read again old Judge Mellon's book, especially the section that begins as follows: "It is much better to form relationships with rising rather than declining families. Where a family has enjoyed their career of wealth and prosperity for a generation or so, we may expect degenerate sons; not invariably, but more frequently than otherwise."

So Thomas Mellon, who had trudged as a poor waif along the dusty country roads on his way to Pittsburgh, past the uncomprehending houses of the rich, so even he had seen the ultimate decay to which great personal wealth led; had seen it, and with a sigh, accepted.

Paul Mellon, in his own idealistic youth, had seen it too, and had glimpsed something else: the rampaging power of corporations, growing and proliferating like some evil plant. He had seen it and recoiled, not from the money that power could buy but from the personal exercise of the power.

His fortune grew largely without him, tended by the zeal of other men. His companies became even more mammoth, surging with a life of their own. They devoured smaller and weaker companies and made a mockery of the word "competition." They invaded the councils of government, like a sinister virus, and they ruled the markets of the world. Foreign governments rose and fell by the power of those companies, and people died in the struggles that ensued.

Paul would say it was not his fault. He neither gives orders nor takes them. He simply exists.

Paul controls thousands of companies. Except for a failed restaurant operation, however, he has never actively run a company.

Hundreds of thousands of people work for him. Except for a few uneventful years at the bank, he has never worked.

He owns the most valuable thoroughbred race horses on earth. He has never ridden in a horse race.

He owns some of the great art masterpieces in the world. He has never painted.

He has given away millions of dollars. He did not earn the money he gave away nor did it cost him a cent to be generous.

189

He owns the manuscripts of many great writers. He has never written a book. But he wanted to be an author.

Paul Mellon collects paintings and donates paintings and watches his race horses run. It would do no good to criticize him, for he could answer as Henry Fielding once did: "Perhaps you will say a man is not young; I answer, he is rich; he is not gentle, handsome, witty, brave, good-humored, but he is rich, rich, rich, rich—that one word contradicts everything you say against him."

Bibliography

Alexander, Robert Jackson. *The Bolivian National Revolution.* New Brunswick, N.J.: Rutgers University Press, 1958.

Amuzegar, Jahangir. *Technical Assistance in Theory and Practice; The Case of Iran.* New York: F. A. Praeger, 1966.

Ball, George W. *The Elements of Our Congo Policy.* Washington: Department of State, 1961.

Belgian Government Information Center, New York. *The Sacred Mission of Civilization; To Which Peoples Should the Benefits be Extended? The Belgian Thesis,* 1953.

Birmingham, David. *The Portuguese Conquest of Angola.* London, New York: Oxford University Press, 1965.

Boyer, Richard O., and Herbert M. Morais. *Labor's Untold Story.* New York: United Electrical, Radio & Machine Workers of America, New York, 1955.

Brill, Wm. Handforth. *Military Intervention in Bolivia: the Overthrow of Paz Estenssoro and the MNR.* Washington: Institute for the Comparative Study of Political Systems, 1967.

British Petroleum Co., Limited. *Persia, Past and Present.* London: Anglo-Iranian Oil Co., 1950.

Calvocoressi, Peter. *South Africa and World Opinion.* London, New York: Oxford University Press, 1961.

Carr, Charles Carl. *Alcoa, an American Enterprise.* New York: Rinehart, 1952.

Castro, Josue de. *Death in the Northeast.* New York: Random House, 1966.

Clark, Joseph W. *Indonesia, Sick Man on the Mend.* Report to the Commission on Foreign Relations, U.S. Senate, on Study Mission to Indonesia. Washington: U.S. Government Printing Office, 1968.

Cook, Fred J. *The Welfare State.* New York: Macmillan, 1962.

Cortissoz, Royal. *An Introduction to the Mellon Collection.* (Priv. printed.) Boston: The Merrymount Press, 1937.

Crist, Raymond E. *Venezuela, Search for a Middle Ground.* New York: Van Nostrand Reinhold, 1969.

Daly, Herman. *The Population Question in Northeast Brazil: Its Economic and Ideological Dimensions.* Baton Rouge: Latin American Studies Institute, Louisiana State University, 1969.

Davenport, Walter. *The Power and the Glory: The Life of Boies Penrose.* New York: Putnam's Sons, 1931.

Davidson, Basil. *The African Awakening.* New York: Macmillan, 1955.

DeKadt, Emanuel J. *Catholic Radicals in Brazil.* London, New York: Oxford University Press, 1970.

Denny, Ludwell. *We Fight for Oil.* New York: Knopf, 1928.

Denton, Frank Richard. *The Mellons of Pittsburgh.* New York: American Branch, Newcomen Society of England, 1948.

Dos Passos, John. *Brazil On the Move.* Garden City, New York: Doubleday, 1963.

Dugauquier, D. *Congo Cauldron.* London: Jarrolds, 1961.

Dulles, John W. F. *Unrest in Brazil, Political-Military Crises.* Austin: University of Texas Press, 1970.

Duncan, Patrick. *South Africa's Rule of Violence.* London: Methuen, 1964.

Egerton, F. Clement C. *Angola in Perspective; Endeavor and Achievement in Portuguese West Africa.* London: Routledge & Paul, 1957.

Ehnmark, Anders. *Angola and Mozambique; the Case Against Portugal.* Translated from the Swedish by Paul Britten-Austin. London: Pall Mall Press, 1963.

Epstein, Howard M., ed. *Revolt in the Congo, 1960–64.* New York: Facts on File, 1965.

Fatemi, Nasrollah Saifpour. *Oil Diplomacy: Powderkeg in Iran.* New York: Whittier Books, 1954.

Fluharty, Vernon Lee. *Dance of the Millions: Military Rule and the Social Revolution in Colombia, 1930–1956.* Pittsburgh: University of Pittsburgh Press, 1957.

Forster, Arnold and Benjamin R. Epstein. *Danger on the Right.* New York: Random House, 1964.

Freyre, Gilberto. *The Mansions and the Shanties; the Making of Modern Brazil.* Translated by S. Putnam. New York: Knopf, 1956.

Gamboa, J. Tavares. *A Short Survey on Angola.* Luanda, Angola: 1965.

Gerassi, John. *North Vietnam, a Documentary.* London: Allen & Unwin, 1968.

————. *The Great Fear in Latin America.* Collier Books, New York; Collier-Macmillan, London, 1963.

Gilchrist, Sidney. *Angola Awake.* Toronto: Ryerson Press, 1968.

Goodrich, Carter. *The Economic Transformation of Bolivia.* Ithaca, N.Y.: State School of Industrial and Labor Relations. Cornell University, 1955.

Griswold, Deirdre. *Indonesia: The Second Greatest Crime of the Century.* New York: World View Publishers, 1970.

Gruening, Ernest. *The Public Pays.* New York: Vanguard, 1931.

Guevara, Ernesto. *Bolivian Diary of Ché Guevara.* Introduction by Fidel Castro. Translated from Spanish by Carlos P. Hansen and Andrew Sinclair, London: Lorrimer Publishers, 1968.

————. *On Vietnam and World Revolution.* Beverly Hills, Calif.: Merit Publishers, 1967.

Hanna, Willard Anderson. *Indonesia, "Guided" Republic.* New York: Foreign Policy Assn., World Affairs Center, 1961.

Harvey, George. *Henry Clay Frick, The Man.* New York: Charles Scribner's Sons, 1928.

Heravi, Mehdi. *Iranian-American Diplomacy.* Brooklyn, N.Y.: T. Gaus Sons, 1969.

Herrick, Allison Butler. *Area Handbook for Angola.* Washington: U.S. Govt. Printing Office, 1967.

Hopkinson, Henry Thomas. *South Africa.* New York: Time, Inc., 1964.

Horowitz, Irving Louis. *Revolution in Brazil; Politics and Society in a Developing Nation.* New York: Dutton, 1964.

Hughes, John. *Indonesian Upheaval.* New York: McKay, 1967.

Hunt, Roy A. *The Aluminum Pioneers.* New York: Newcomen Society in North America, 1951.

Hyde, Douglas Arnold. *Confrontation in the East, a Background Book.* Dufour Eds., Chester Springs, Pa.: 1965.

Institute of Race Relations. *Angola: A Symposium; Views of a Revolt.* London, New York: Oxford University Press, 1962.

Inter-American Development Commission. *Technical Mission to Paraguay.* Washington, D.C., 1946.

International Labor Office. *Report to Government of State of Kuwait on the Vocational Training of Adult Workers.* Geneva, 1962.

In Support of the People of the Congo (Leopoldville) Against U.S. Aggression. Peking: Foreign Languages Press, 1965.

Jack, Homer Alexander. *Angola: Repression and Revolt in Portuguese Africa.* New York: American Commission on Africa, 1960.

James, Harold. *The Undeclared War: The Story of the Indonesian Confrontation.* London: Leo Cooper, 1971.

James, Herman Gerlach. *The Constitutional System of Brazil.* Washington, D.C.: The Carnegie Institute of Washington, 1923.

Jones, Howard Palfredy. *Indonesia: The Possible Dream.* New York: Harcourt, Brace, Jovanovich, 1971.

Kahn, Otto Hermann. *Why I Favor the Mellon Tax Plan.* Distributed by the Citizens National Commission in support of the Mellon Tax Reduction Proposal, New York: 1924.

Kendrick, Alexander. *Prime Time, The Life of Edward R. Murrow.* Boston: Little, Brown & Co., 1969.

Latrobe, Ferdinand C. *Iron Men and Their Dogs.* Baltimore: Ivan R. Drechler, 1941.

Legum, Collin. *Congo Disaster.* Baltimore: Penguin Books, 1961.

Lindahl, Martin L. and Wm. A. Carter. *Corporate Concentration and Public Policy.* Englewood Cliffs, N. J.: Prentice-Hall, Inc., 1959.

Loeb (Carl M.), Rhoades & Co. New York: *Aluminum, an Analysis of the Industry in the U.S.*

Long, Luman H., ed. *The World Almanac, 1973 Edition.* New York: Newspaper Enterprise Assn., Inc., 1973.

Love, Philip H. *Andrew W. Mellon, The Man and His Work.* Baltimore: F. H. Coggins & Co., 1929.

Lowenstein, James G. *Vietnam, Dec. 1969.* Staff Report for Committee on Foreign Relations, U.S. Senate. Washington: U.S. Government Printing Office, 1970.

Lundberg, Ferdinand. *America's 60 Families.* New York: The Citadel Press, 1946.

————. *The Rich and the Super-Rich, A Study in the Power of Money Today.* New York: Lyle Stuart, 1968.

MacPhail, Ian. *Alchemy and the Occult: a Catalogue of Books and Manuscripts from the Collection of Paul and Mary Mellon Given to Yale.* Rare Book Collection, Library of Congress, Washington, D.C.

Malloy, James M. *Bolivia: The Uncompleted Revolution.* Pittsburgh: Pittsburgh University Press, 1970.

Manchester, William. *The Death of a President.* New York: Harper & Row, 1967.

Marcum, John. *The Angolan Revolution.* Cambridge, Mass.: Massachusetts Institute of Technology Press, 1969.

Martelli, George. *Leopold to Lumumba, A History of the Belgian Congo, 1877–1960.* London: Chapman & Hall, 1962.

Martz, John D. *Colombia: A Contemporary Political Survey.* Chapel Hill: University of North Carolina Press, 1962.

Mellon, A. W. *Taxation: The People's Business.* New York: The Macmillan Co., 1924.

Mellon, James Ross. *Letters.* Pittsburgh: Stevenson and Foster Co., 1935.

Mellon National Bank and Trust Company, Pittsburgh. *A Brief Historical Sketch of the Bank, Beginning with its Founding by Thomas Mellon in 1869.* Pittsburgh: 1946, in observance of its 75th year.

Mellon, Thomas. *Thomas Mellon and His Times; Printed for his Family and Descendants Exclusively.* Pittsburgh: W. G. Johnston & Co., 1885.

Mellon, Thomas, Jr. *Army "Y" Diary.* Pittsburgh: The Crescent Press, 1920.

Mellon, William Larimer. *Judge Mellon's Sons.* B. Sparks collaborator. Pittsburgh: Private Printing, 1948.

Melman, Seymour. *Our Depleted Society.* New York. Holt, Rinehart and Winston, 1965.

Melo, Antonio. *The Coming Revolution in Brazil.* Translation and introduction by R. Menzel. New York: Exposition Press, 1970.

Mezerik, Avrahm G. *The Role of Oil in the Middle East.* New York: International Review Service, 1961.

Minty, Abdul S. *South Africa's Defence Strategy.* Introduction by Rt. Rev. Trevor Huddleston, Anti-Apartheid Movement. London: 1969.

Missen, David. *Iran: Oil at the Service of the Nation.* London: Transorient, 1969.

Muller, Charlotte (Feldman). *Light Metals Monopoly.* New York: AMS Press, 1968.

Myers, Gustavus. *History of the Great American Fortunes.* New York: The Modern Library, 1907, 1936.

Nkrumah, Kwame. *Challenge of the Congo.* New York: International Publishers, 1967.

O'Connor, Harvey. *Empire of Oil.* New York: Monthly Review Press, 1955.

———. *Mellon's Millions, The Biography of a Fortune: The Life and Times of Andrew Mellon.* New York: Blue Ribbon Books, 1933.

———. *World Crisis in Oil.* New York: Monthly Review Press, 1962.

Okuma, Thomas. *Angola in Ferment, The Background and Prospects of Angolan Nationalism.* Boston: Beacon Press, 1962.

O'Shaughnessy, Michael J. *Venezuelan Oil Fields, Developments to September 1924.* New York: 1924.

Pahlavi, Mohammed Reza, Shah of Iran. *The White Revolution of Iran.* Tehran: Imperial Pahlavi Library, 1967.

Panikkar, K. M. *Angola in Flames.* New York: Asia Publishing House, 1962.

Patman, Wright. *Banketeering, Bonuseering, Melloneering.* Paris, Texas: Peerless Printing Co., 1934.

Paton, Alan. *South Africa in Transition*. New York: Scribner, 1956.

————. *The People Wept. A brief account of the origin, contents and application of that unjust law of the Union of S. Africa known as the Group Areas Act of 1950, since consolidated as Act No. 77 of 1957.*

Payne, James L. *Patterns of Conflict in Colombia*. New Haven: Yale University Press, 1968.

Perlo, Victor. *The Empire of High Finance*. New York: International Publishers, 1957.

Peterson, Robert W., ed. *South Africa and Apartheid*. New York: Facts on File, 1971.

Portuguese-American Commission on Foreign Affairs. *The Communists and Angola*. Boston: 1961.

Reisky, Dubnic, Vladimir. *Political Trends in Brazil*. Foreword by A. Berle. Washington: Public Affairs Press, 1968.

Rippy, J. Fred. *The Capitalists and Colombia*. New York: Vanguard, 1931.

Rosenberg, Milton J. *Vietnam and the Silent Majority*. New York: Harper & Row, 1970.

Rosenthal, Eric. *South Africa's Oil Search Down the Years*. Cape Town: H. Timmins, 1970.

Scott, Sir Ian. *Tumbled House: The Congo at Independence*. New York: Oxford University Press, 1969.

Schlesinger, Arthur. *The Bitter Heritage: Vietnam and American Democracy*. Boston: Houghton-Mifflin, 1967.

Seldes, George. *One Thousand Americans*. New York: Boni & Gaer, 1947.

Shannon, Jasper B. *Money and Politics*. New York: Random House, 1959.

Sheehan, Michael K. *Iran: The Impact of U.S. Interests and Policies, 1941–1954*. Brooklyn: Gaus and Sons, 1968.

Smith, Thomas Lynn. *Colombia: Social Structure and the Process of Development*. Foreword by Alberto Lleras Gainesville: University of Florida Press, 1967.

198

Statham, Francis R. *South Africa as It Is*. New York: Negro Universities Press, 1969.

Standard Oil Co. *Standard Oil and Middle-East Production: Background Memorandum*. New York: Standard Oil of New Jersey, 1954.

Tams, Georg. *Visit to the Portuguese Possessions in Southwestern Africa*. Translated from the German by H. Evans Lloyd. New York: Negro University Press, 1969.

Teixeira, Bernardo. *The Fabric of Terror: Three Days in Angola*. Introduction by Robt. Ruark. New York: Devin-Adair Co., 1965.

Thayer, Mary Van Rensselaer. *Jacqueline Kennedy: The White House Years*. Boston: Little, Brown & Co., 1967.

Thompson, Craig. *Since Spindletop: A Human Story of Gulf's First Half-Century*. Pittsburgh, 1951.

United Nations, General Assembly, Subcommittee on the Situation in Angola, *Report*, New York: 1961.

U.S. Bureau of Labor Statistics. *Wage Chronology: Aluminum Company of America, 1939–1950*. Washington. Reprinted from the Bureau's Monthly Labor Review.

U.S. Department of Justice. 1912. *Aluminum Co. of America, Report of Special Asst. to the Attorney General., Wm. R. Benham.*

U.S. General Accounting Office. 1963. *Report of Comptroller General to Congress*. Washington. Concerns non-competitive procurement of military aircraft forgings from Alcoa at higher prices than current and expected.

U.S. General Accounting Office. 1963. *Report of Comptroller General to the Congress*. Washington. Procurement of aluminum caps and cans without adequate pricing data by General Electric from Alcoa under AEC contracts.

U.S. General Accounting Office. 1964. *Report of Comptroller General to the Congress*. Washington. On pricing of weapons components.

U.S. General Accounting Office. 1964. *Report of Comptroller General to the Congress.* Washington. Overpricing of reactor weldments.

U.S. House of Representatives, Staff Report for the Subcommittee on Domestic Finance, Committee on Banking and Currency, 90th Congress, 2d session. *Commercial Banks and Their Trust Activities: Emerging Influence on the American Economy.* 2 vols.

U.S. National Gallery of Art. *An Exhibition of English Drawings and Water Colors from the collection of Mr. and Mrs. Paul Mellon.* Feb. 18-Apr. 1, 1962, Washington.

U.S. Senate, Committee on the Judiciary. 1932. *Eligibility of Hon. Andrew W. Mellon, Secretary of the Treasury.*

U.S. Senate, Committee on the Judiciary. 1926. *The Department of Justice and the Aluminum Co. of America.* Minority Report.

U.S. Senate, Committee on the Judiciary. Jan. 1926. *Hearings on Aluminum Co. of America.*

U.S. Senate, Committee on Government Operations, *War Assets Administration sale of Koppers plant, Hearings before Investigating Subcommittee* (sale of war plant) Nov. 8, 1948.

U.S. Tariff Commission. *Mining and Manufacturing Industries in Paraguay.* Washington, United States Tariff Commission, 1946.

Van den Berghe, Pierre L. *South Africa, a Study in Conflict,* Middletown, Conn.: Wesleyan University Press, 1965.

Vandenbosch, A. *South Africa and the World: The Foreign Policy of Apartheid.* Lexington: University of Kentucky Press, 1970.

Venter, A. J. *The Terror Fighters: A Profile of Guerrilla Warfare in Southern Africa.* Cape Town, Johannesburg: Purnell, 1969.

Villarroel, C. R. *Bolivia.* English translation by Ralph Dimmick. Washington: Pan American Union, 1963.

Weatherbee, Donald E. *Ideology: Sukarno's Indonesian Revolution.* New Haven: Southeast Asia Studies, Yale University, 1966.

Wendel, Wm. H. *The Scratch Heard 'Round the World: The Story of the Carborundum Company.* New York: Newcomen Society in North America, 1965.

Wheeler, Douglas L. *Angola.* New York: Praeger Publishers, 1971.

Wilkie, James W. *The Bolivian Revolution and U.S. Aid since 1952.* Los Angeles: Latin American Center, University of Calif., 1969.

Wise, David and Ross, Thomas B. *The Invisible Government.* New York: Random House, 1964.

Young, Crawford. *Politics in the Congo: Decolonization and Independence.* Princeton, N. J.: Princeton University Press, 1965.

Zondas, Cornelius H. *The Bolivian Economy, 1952–65: The Revolution and its Aftermath.* New York: Praeger, 1966.

PERIODICALS

Bookman, George. "Alcoa Strikes Back." *Fortune,* November 1962, pp. 114-119.

Kay, Hubert. "The Third Force in Urban Renewal." *Fortune,* October 1964, p. 130.

Kubly, Hubert. "Pittsburgh." *Holiday,* March 1959, pp. 80-87.

Rieser, Carl. "The Distribution Upheaval IV: The Short-Order Economy." *Fortune,* August 1962, pp. 90-95.

Schoenbrun, David. "David Bruce: 'Amateur Professional'." *New York Times Magazine,* 16 April 1961, p. 30.

Visson, Andre. "Three-Star Ambassador." *Reader's Digest,* November 1961, pp. 222-224.

"Alcoa Jumps Across the Ocean." *Business Week,* 27 June 1959, p. 34.

"Alcoa Makes Way for Younger Men." *Business Week,* 25 April 1959, p. 156.

"Alcoa's British Tie-in Stirs Outcry." *Business Week,* 6 December 1958, p. 18.

"Alcoa's Man Magee." *Newsweek,* 26 September 1960, pp. 93-94.

"Aluminum's Paradox in Prices." *Business Week,* 1 February 1964, p. 21.

"Andrew Mellon on Tax Cuts." *New Republic,* 23 March 1963, p. 22.

"Antitrust Law Hits Aluminum." *Business Week,* 6 June 1964, p. 98.

"Argentina: A Cold Shoulder to Foreign Oil Giants." *Business Week,* 17 June 1972, p. 48.

"A Second String to Alcoa's Bow." *Business Week,* 24 November 1962, p. 82.

"Back to the Ould Sod." *Time,* 28 June 1968, pp. 48-50.

"Behind the Latest Arab Oil Seizure." *U.S. News and World Report,* 12 June 1972, p. 84.

"Big Porcelain Cake in Oven for Atomic Research." *Business Week,* 5 September 1959, pp. 78-81.

"Big Steel Gets Jump in Canadian Ore Race." *Business Week,* 28 January 1961, p. 62.

"Breaking a Pattern of Woes." *Business Week,* 31 August 1963, p. 90.

"Business Roundup." *Fortune,* June 1952, p. 27.

"David K. E. Bruce: A Europe-Centered Secretary." *New Republic,* 14 November 1960, p. 4.

"Dim Profits, Bright Hopes at Alcoa." *Business Week,* 16 April 1960, pp. 168-170.

"Dumping Dispute." *Time,* 26 April 1963, p. 86.

"Educated Crystals." *Time,* 1 February 1960, p. 54.

"Executive Pay Takes a Breather." *Business Week,* 16 April 1960, p. 174.

"Executive: The Blue Chips." *Newsweek,* 4 May 1959, p. 78.

"Fertilizing the Oil Business." *Time,* 20 September 1963, p. 92.

"Genius Defined." *Time,* 5 July 1963, p. 58.

"Good Gulf Citizenship." *Newsweek,* 20 July 1959, p. 100.

"Iraq's Stormy Petrol: Nationalization of Iraq Petroleum Company." *Time,* 19 June 1972, pp. 77-78.

"IUE Seeks Contract Breakthrough." *Business Week,* 16 July 1960, pp. 47-48.

"Mellon Bank Steps Down from its Pedestal." *Business Week,* 1 June 1963, p. 108.

"Model City on Old Movie Lots." *Business Week,* 22 April 1961, pp. 123-124.

"Mopping up After Antitrust Suits." *Business Week,* 28 January 1961, p. 35.

"Mr. Automation." *Time,* 26 July 1963, p. 73.

"Mrs. David K. E. Bruce, Wife of the American Ambassador to Great Britain." *Vogue,* May 1961, p. 131.

'Mrs. Paul Mellon's Garden in Virginia." *Vogue,* July 1962, pp. 52-55.

"New Envoy to Britain." *U.S. News and World Report,* 13 February 1961, p. 20.

"New Gasolines Stir up a Storm." *Business Week,* 25 November 1961, pp. 83-84.

"New Power Source Goes to Work." *Business Week,* 21 January 1961, p. 52.

"Oil Import Suit: Gulf Asks Court to Block Government Enforcement of Restriction on Foreign Residual Brought into the U.S." *Business Week,* 23 April 1966, p. 34.

"Oil on Ocean Beaches: A Growing Worry." *U.S. News and World Report,* 18 March 1968, p. 19.

"Pittsburgh Rebuilds." *Fortune,* June 1952, p. 88.

"Pittsburgh Splits over Skybus." *Business Week,* 7 August 1971, p. 25.

"Power Reactor Makers Launch Business Drive." *Business Week,* 14 March 1964, p. 43.

"President, Plus." *Newsweek,* 13 April 1959, p. 82.

"Return of the Natives." *Newsweek,* 1 July 1968, pp. 51-52.

"Russia's Game in Mideast Oil Fields." *U.S. News and World Report,* 26 June 1972, pp. 52-53.

"Sonics and Steel: Westinghouse Is Evolving a Method by Which Sonic Waves Are Used to Make the Fanciest Ingots Even Fancier." *Business Week,* June 13, 1959, pp. 78–79.

"Speed-up on the Campus." *Newsweek,* 7 August 1961, pp. 70-71.

"Steel and Aluminum Vie for Containers." *Business Week,* 13 October 1962, p. 60.

"The Art Market: Parke-Bernet Opens a New West Wing." *Business Week,* 27 February 1971, p. 39.

"The Money Men." *Forbes,* 1 January 1972, p. 89.

"Tight Financial Controls Are Key: How Westinghouse Pulled up its Profit Margin." *Business Week,* 19 November 1960, p. 98.

"Trying to Untangle a Price Snarl." *Business Week,* 7 December 1963, p. 81.

"Turbine Price Cuts, but no War." *Business Week,* 18 July 1959, p. 32.

"Wait a minute: Let's Not Go Overboard on Ecology." Adaptation of address, July 15, 1971, Maurice H. Stans. *Reader's Digest,* January 1972, pp. 114-118.

"Westinghouse Cracks the Nuclear Power Market." *Business Week,* 13 November 1971, p. 58.